Caitlin & S

Enjoy and thank

you for all you

are already doing

to serve!

ENDORSEMENTS

"This is one of those rare and wonderful books that has the ability to transform your business and personal success. I highly recommend it."

—KEITH FERRAZZI, *NEW YORK TIMES* BEST-SELLING AUTHOR OF *NEVER EAT ALONE*

"How's this for a business strategy? Do good deeds for every person you meet and don't ask for or expect anything in return. Sound crazy? Then read this book. Jonathan Keyser has built his whole company around "selfless service," and it has worked brilliantly."

—BO BURLINGHAM, FORMER *INC.* EDITOR, *FORBES* CONTRIBUTOR, AND BEST-SELLING AUTHOR OF *SMALL GIANTS* AND *FINISH BIG*

"This book is a field commander's guide to accumulating wealth through service, and I will not be surprised if every single person who can read will one day have read this book."

—STEVE CHANDLER, NBC CONTRIBUTOR, AUTHOR, SPEAKER, AND MASTER COACH

"Reading this book has been like putting the missing coordinates into my life's GPS and hitting GO!"

—GARY MAHLER, AUTHOR, SPEAKER, AND EXECUTIVE BUSINESS COACH

"Business is changing. It doesn't have to be ruthless, and thankfully, Jonathan Keyser is showing us another way."

—JOHN MACKEY, CEO AND CO-FOUNDER OF WHOLE FOODS MARKET

YOU DON'T HAVE TO BE

RUTHLESS

TO WIN

JONATHAN KEYSER

My Disclaimer: My story and examples within these pages are relayed to the best of my remembrance at the time. As someone who has learned to live in the moment, some of the timelines, details, people, or representations may be out of order, remembered differently by others, or simply inaccurate. It is not intentional, as I truly did relay my journey to the best of my remembrance.

Additionally, some items within have actually been altered intentionally to keep the people, stories, and recommendations confidential.

Lastly, this is a story about my journey and philosophy around how to create success through service. While I believe wholeheartedly in our approach and philosophy and have personally created success through service, there is no guarantee that the ideas, strategies, and recommendations employed within will guarantee success for you or anyone else. If you are interested in truly reinventing yourself around service and you feel like you would like additional assistance, call us, and we will help you however we can.

YOU DON'T HAVE TO BE RUTHLESS TO WIN

The Art of Badass Selfless Service

ISBN   978-1-5445-0426-1 *Hardcover*

978-1-5445-0424-7 *Paperback*

978-1-5445-0425-4 *Ebook*

978-1-5445-0427-8 *Audiobook*

LIONCREST
PUBLISHING

For my beloved children: Jonathan, Ulysses, Finnegan, and London.

*Each one of you is a priceless gift, and I am
honored and humbled to be your dad.*

*The joy of being your father is my greatest
blessing, and I am forever enriched by you.*

*You are each extraordinary, uniquely talented,
loving, selfless, and kind; I am the luckiest guy in
the world to be able to call you my kiddos.*

*Each of you is perfect exactly as you are. Don't ever be
anything other than your true self. There is only one you,
perfect and priceless and infinitely powerful, so never try to
be anyone else or anything other than your own perfect self.*

*Follow your heart at all times, and never forget
who you are and what you are capable of.*

*In dark times, remember that your dad loves you
unconditionally, and nothing any of you could ever do could
change that. I will always be here for you when you need me.*

*Thank you for having the generosity and grace to forgive and
love me despite the many times that I have failed as a dad
and not showed you unconditional love and selfless service.*

*My wish for each and every one of you is that you will find
for yourselves the joy and power in living a life of service to
others, and that it will transform your lives as it has mine.*

CONTENTS

PART TWO: CREATING THE KEYSER EXPERIENCE FOR YOURSELF

"Only a life lived in service to others is worth living."

—ALBERT EINSTEIN

AN INVITATION

I envision a world—

A world in which business people selflessly help one another and, as a direct result, achieve extraordinary levels of success.

A world where the brightest graduates from the best universities transform the companies that hire them through selfless service.

A world where business people focus 100 percent of their efforts on selflessly helping their clients, colleagues, and other business leaders succeed. As a result, they achieve unusually high levels of success for themselves simply because they helped other people.

A world in which everyone lives by the mantra "Give, and you shall receive."

This may seem unrealistic, but I believe it is indeed possible. In fact, we are proving it every day in one of the most ruthless industries in the world.

I invite you to join me in the expansion of one of the most unlikely, yet phenomenally effective, approaches to business you'll ever see.

I had been in the industry for ten years. Ten years. And I had lost myself in the backstabbing drudge of it all.

I had started the same way anyone does in the commercial real estate business—at the bottom, scratching up business wherever I could get it, making cold calls, trying to survive off a commission-based income. But after ten years, even with the financial success I was experiencing, nothing felt right.

It was in the last two of those years that I began to reinvent myself—I wanted to do business differently. I had heard about the concept of selfless service during a breakout session at a business conference, and I couldn't let it go. I dug in deep, researched, hunted down others who were practicing this method, and even took on a coach to help me internalize the process. While I was starting to see some success, a brick wall had planted itself firmly in front of me.

I was doing "others first" work in a "take all you can get"

world. While I was finally feeling good about the work I was doing and beginning to make headway, the endless sound of their mockery echoed in my mind: "No one can survive doing business by just helping others." It was getting harder to stay focused, harder to stay the course. Friends, family, other business leaders in the community, and even people within my firm at the time were convinced I would fail.

I began to avoid going into the office and started working from home or from my car. My sleep was restless, and the stress was becoming unbearable. All I could hear were the voices of people repeatedly telling me I would never make it.

One morning, I woke up in despair and called my coach, Steve Chandler. I hadn't met with him for a while at this point, but I needed to talk to someone. He agreed to meet with me, so I drove out to his office, and as I sat down, he asked, "So, what's going on?" I just couldn't do it anymore. I am not usually a crier, but I was so frustrated that I broke down, unloading all the frustration and anxiety I had been holding back. In that moment, the strain was so great that I broke into uncontrollable sobs. I was at my wit's end, up against relentless opposition and surrounded by critics, and I didn't know what to do. My head was filled with constant concern that I would lose my job, and I didn't feel I could keep going.

Steve listened. He waited. Then he reminded me of the advice he'd already given me and said, "You need to call Steve Hardison. He'll help you do something about this. He'll help you move to the next level—then you'll look back at this moment and recognize it as your turning point. Your life will never be the same."

A WORLD I DIDN'T "GET"

Success was my constant desire after growing up poor. Our family was always one step away from losing our home to the bank, and sometimes we even lacked the ability to buy basic necessities. I became determined to find a way to become successful in my life.

Growing up, my parents taught me to be of selfless service to others, and I naively thought this was how business operated as well. I began my professional career like everyone else, with dreams of success and ideas about how business and relationships should work. As you can imagine, I had a rude awakening and realized that the world of big business operated very differently from how I was raised.

While I wanted to believe that my parents were right in their service orientation, they had never experienced any real form of material success. So, in my thinking, I saw no other explanation than that they just didn't "get" what it took to be successful.

I found that people in the commercial real estate industry had no concept whatsoever of serving others. Instead, they were fighting, scratching, and clawing for themselves, ruthlessly grabbing every opportunity they could find. It seemed like winning at any cost was the rule of the game. They often undercut fellow team members by manipulating conversations or lying to get a bigger share of the transaction. Brokers pulled clients away from their own coworkers, competing within their own companies. I remember hearing of an agent whose son had gotten sick and needed help, and so the agent asked his partner to take a meeting for him. The partner went into the meeting with his own résumé and influenced the client to hire him as the lead instead, and he ended up getting the larger commission.

When I got into the business of commercial real estate brokerage, a business that was 100 percent commission based, it appeared that in order for me to survive I would have to adapt to this ruthless and competitive environment; and that's *exactly* what I did.

I wanted to get ahead, and if that type of behavior is what it took, then I was going to do it. You see, I thought it was the only way. For years, I lived my adult life doing my best to excel in the highly competitive dog-eat-dog world of commercial real estate. I was manipulative and ruthless, and I did whatever was necessary to win, regardless of the collateral damage it caused.

But happiness was never part of the picture. I was stressed out and constantly looking over my shoulder, painfully aware that my behavior was fundamentally misaligned with my core values and beliefs.

CRAZY CHANGE

I didn't realize then how abruptly change would hit me. When I attended a business conference in Miami, I was introduced to a radical new business approach centered on focusing all one's efforts on helping others succeed. This strategy resonated with my selfless-service upbringing. Deciding to abandon my ruthless tactics and pursue this maverick new approach, I began the difficult process of reinventing myself.

To many über-competitive business people I spoke to about it, the idea of "being successful by helping as many other people succeed as possible" sounded insane and financially irresponsible—and in many cases, it still does. Nevertheless, I decided to spend all my time figuring out how I could help other business people rather than calling on companies and trying to sell them on hiring me. Rather than looking for clients all day for myself, I decided to try to find ways to help everyone I interacted with be more successful. This personal "reinvention" totally changed my focus and was a 180-degree shift from all I had learned coming up through the ranks of commercial real estate brokerage.

As crazy as that dramatic shift in my approach looked to everyone around me at the time, the truth is this: helping others succeed is the best business strategy I have ever seen for creating long-term sustainable success. I made that commitment in 2005, and I have never looked back.

This concept may sound crazy and even silly or naive to many of you. As a highly driven, type A personality, I can understand. I can tell you, however—based on actually doing it and creating success beyond what I ever imagined—that it is an extraordinary way to become successful. I don't have to sell. I don't have to persuade. I don't have to convince. I just serve, and more business comes my way than I can handle.

Sound too good to be true? Good. You are paying attention. I wrote this book to show the skeptic in you that The Keyser Way is not only a better way to do business, but it is also the best way to make so much money that you won't know what to do with it all; *and* along the way, you will also find happiness and joy in your life in the process as a by-product of selflessly serving others.

A WAY OF LIFE AND BUSINESS

Changing your business approach to the method I teach within this book may sound daunting at first, but I am here to tell you that you can do it, just as I have. I am an ordinary person. I may have more motivation than many, but I am no smarter nor more talented, to be sure. I didn't grow up with family connections, and I had to study much harder than most of my college classmates to get good grades. Yet, to my own surprise and the surprise of many others, Keyser has already grown, and we are well on our way with a clear vision to become the largest and most successful corporate real estate and business consulting firm in the country.

If I, a formerly ruthless and self-serving commercial real estate broker, can make this transformation, *anyone* can. It was sometimes difficult to stick with this disruptive way of doing business as I saw others making quick commissions ruthlessly; however, it came surprisingly more easily than I expected. I also found that over time, my partners and clients fell in love with my new way of doing business and wanted to work with me even more than they had before.

But let me be clear. The service-first methodology that I teach you within these pages is not an instant-gratification model. This is not the "make money quick" way to do business; it takes years to truly see the results. But if you remain committed to the model and keep serving, the payback you see over time will be nothing short of phenomenal, and if I may be so bold, you will never have to sell again.

PART / ONE

A JOURNEY TO SELFLESSNESS

Within this book, I condense all of the secrets and lessons I have learned over my twenty-year business career so that you, the reader, have all the tools you need to create extraordinary success through service in your own organization. I want you to have the ability to learn from my failures and successes so you can do for yourself within your chosen industry what I have done in commercial real estate brokerage. This is not a ten-year plan for success but rather a detailed strategy that you can act on now. Today.

Whether you are new to business, have been a business leader for a few years now, or you are a senior business leader with thirty years of experience running dozens of companies all around the world, this book is for you.

This book explains both the *why* of doing business the way we do as well as the *how*. It explains specific strategies for putting this daring proposition into practice, and it teaches the guiding Principles by which we operate here at Keyser.

Part One begins with my story. I am sharing my story because I want you to understand what it actually took for me to implement this model so you have a real-life example to follow. There are very few people in business actually living this selfless service model, but there are millions who write or speak about it. I am not one of those talking heads. I am a company leader like you, and I am actively building and growing a successful company using the strategies outlined within. This isn't theory. This is philosophy in action, and we are proving it works every day in our company.

As you read through each chapter, you will see why and how my new way of operating came into being. The unique methodology I use has not only given me amazing financial success, but it has also brought me great joy and created extraordinary relationships that otherwise would never have been possible. It has inspired me to change an industry through service, and most importantly, it has helped me sleep much better at night knowing I am help-ing people rather than manipulating them.

So take your time. Pay attention. Learn from my jour-ney, and allow yourself to see my experiences for what they are—the path that led me to fully understand how to create extraordinary success through service, even within an industry as ruthless and cutthroat as commercial real estate brokerage.

If I can do it in commercial real estate brokerage, you can do it in any industry.

Then, in Part Two, I will unfold for you the simple but profound three-level process to reinvention that you as a business leader can use to create The Keyser Experience within your own organization.

Through the Three Levels of Reinvention laid out in detail within the framework of Keyser's 15 Core Operating Principles, I will teach you step by step how to create a successful culture of service for yourself. I want to enable you to transform your own life and business into a masterpiece utilizing my philosophies. If you trust the process and take it one step at a time—beginning within yourself—your future will be unstoppable and extraordinary.

The bottom line is that this book is really about you. I wrote it to provide you with the motivation, strategy, and tools to transform yourself and your organization through service. May this book inspire and equip you to experience extraordinary success.

Thank you for taking a chance on my story. I promise, you will not regret it.

CHAPTER 1

GROWING UP SELFLESS WITHOUT A CHOICE

I grew up as a Christian missionary kid in Papua New Guinea (PNG), of all places. (You might need to get out your world map to find it.) I grew up in a home where our whole lives were about helping others. My parents were constantly looking for ways to serve others—from bringing meals to families, to providing rides for people who didn't have transportation, to putting money at Christmastime into a little gift box and taking it to a refugee family. We provided a place to stay for many of those around us having a tough time, and our doors were always open to those in need.

We met some very interesting people during our time there. Many of those experiences added to the examples

I had of welcoming and loving every person, even the more challenging ones. I remember one guy who came to stay at our home for a couple of days. He was a very odd and socially awkward American in his twenties who had just made a daylong trek through the jungle and needed a place to rest up. It turned out that he was a vegetarian. While that is commonplace today, back then, I don't think my parents had ever met a true vegetarian.

For dinner that first night, my mom made a nice meal to share with this man. He sat down at the table and, seeing animal products on his plate, pushed his plate away dramatically and told my mom in a loud, disgusted voice he couldn't eat any of it. My mom didn't react negatively but instead put a smile on her face, got up, and went out to the garden to get something different to prepare for him. He was a very odd guy and didn't show any appreciation for her extra effort once his "acceptable" meal was brought out to him.

As kids, watching him, we felt quite nervous having him in our house, but my parents showed him love and welcomed him.

Even without much money, I learned the values of giving, loving, serving, and putting others first. I saw that it gave my parents the joy, satisfaction, and fulfillment that comes with helping others. In their minds, they were wealthy. They considered the needs of hurting people they saw around them as much greater than their own.

THEY CHOSE TO SERVE

My mother had grown up as a missionary kid herself on the Apache Indian Reservation in Arizona, living among people who were extremely poor. She decided at a young age that helping people was far more important to her than having a lot of money. My dad also felt that way, and he had specifically chosen missionary and church work as his career over corporate finance, wanting to spend his life simply serving others.

For me, it was a different story.

From the ages of seven through eleven, my family lived in PNG, where my younger sister and I were the only missionary kids in a very remote, mountainous area in the middle of nowhere. We were—by far—the richest kids around, compared to the local children who lived in grass huts and typically had one set of clothes apiece, if they had any. Many of my local friends wore only bush materials to cover themselves. Their "toys" consisted of sticks and stones and old tires, and they went hungry more often than not. So even though we had very little ourselves by US standards, I had many opportunities to share, and I had more than most.

There were a few things that I desperately wanted, though. I wanted and dreamed about having a bike constantly. Every six months or so, a large wooden crate would arrive with donations for us missionaries, and we would all crowd around it looking for toys or clothes that would fit us. Each time, I anxiously looked to see if there was a bike inside, and each time I was disappointed.

Then, one day, we opened the crate and, sure enough, there was a bike! It was my size and everything. I was so excited—that is, until I realized that it had only one pedal. The highlands of New Guinea didn't have bike stores where we could run over and grab a pedal. I was crushed. I tried everything, from jamming in twigs and sticks trying to make it work, to having one of the other missionaries try to weld a metal pole to the bike for another pedal. But it all led back to disappointment. So close yet so far away!

Despite not having a workable bike, I didn't really have an overall sense of lack there because of the poverty surrounding me. However, it was when we returned to the United States that I really understood how poor we were according to US standards. I realized in a sobering flash that I didn't have what the other American kids had. My mom literally cut my hair using a bowl. I only had mismatched, often dorky, hand-me-down clothes from thrift stores or the missionary box, and we had no money to buy any of the cool stuff that all the other kids seemed to have.

It was difficult growing up in a home where my parents praying for enough money to pay the bills was the norm. To me, the life of service and giving was what kept us poor. I didn't understand their reasons, and feelings of frustration grew within me. I decided then that I did not want to live the way they had taught me. I did not want to constantly give and be selfless only to be poor, and I did not want my kids someday to have to experience what I was going through.

I realize now that these life experiences were a gift to me. They taught me two things: (1) to understand the disappointment of having a need go unmet and (2) to know the joy of receiving from someone who gave to meet my need. The lessons I have learned from growing up poor have been priceless.

AN EXAMPLE TO FOLLOW

My dearest mother is like a saint and is the most selfless person I have ever met. She is where I learned how to sit down and truly listen to people, to hear them, to wrap my entire being around what the person is saying and feeling—that entire mindset came from my sweet mom. She is giving, generous, and extraordinary in every way. Everyone who has met her knows she is pure love, endlessly positive, and unconditionally caring of everyone she meets. She is my hero.

When I was a kid, everyone loved my mom. Because of her, our house was the place where kids in the neighborhood wanted to come. When they were at our house, my mom became their mom. She loved them all, and they had nothing but love and respect for her. She did everything in her power to make sure her presence was one of unconditional acceptance and care for each of them. Her unconditional love for people gave me the foundation of love and respect for others that I carry forward into my company. Our office is modeled to be a place both brokers and companies with real estate needs want to be a part of and where they feel unconditional acceptance and care.

When I am faced with difficulties, I often think, "What would Mom do?" And then I do exactly that. When she's been attacked or disrespected, I have never seen her get angry or offended. She cares far too much about the other person and their feelings. Rather than taking insults personally, she responds with love and empathy, knowing that only people struggling with unhappiness would attack someone else. She has always been an incredible example in my life.

A FOUNDATION OF SELFLESS SERVICE

My father, too, is an example of service. He puts others first and is loving and caring. He's always available to serve those around him. My dad and I are two strong, type A personalities, and we had our fair share of conflict while I was growing up. I now see that all the things that really frustrated me about my dad when I was a child were part of his gift to me. He taught me important concepts that are needed to be successful in life. At the time, I was too blind to see it.

My dad always prioritized his family, which he did even at the expense of his own dreams and goals—but I'll get to that example later. It is because of his dedication to us that one of my goals when I created Keyser was to show him that his investment in me had been worth the time, money, pain, and effort of raising me.

Because there were so many years of financial struggle for my family, I was able to experience both sides of giving.

Sometimes we were the givers, and other times we were the receivers. I know the feeling of both.

My parents introduced and formed the foundation of selfless service in my life. I was exposed to this transformative principle through their daily actions. These are the people who started me out on my journey and, ultimately, the ones who made that journey possible. The things they taught me about love and serving others would eventually come full circle and create extraordinary financial success in my own life.

I just didn't know it at the time.

CHAPTER 2

LEAVING A LEGACY

This legacy of serving didn't start with my parents. It began a full generation earlier with my maternal grandparents. They bravely raised eight children in a tiny trailer on the Apache Indian Reservation in San Carlos, Arizona, while my grandfather worked as part of a team that translated the Bible into the Apache language and founded and led a local church. My grandfather felt that he had been called to serve the Apache people, and he dedicated his entire life relentlessly to his work.

DESIRING MORE

The opportunity to serve in PNG was a dream come true for my parents. While my mom homeschooled my sister and me, my dad created a Bible curriculum for the local church leaders in their language to train their own pastors, helping them to free themselves of their dependence on the missionaries.

When I was eleven and still in PNG, my grandfather back home in the United States died unexpectedly, so our family left PNG and flew home for his funeral. At that time, I was just finishing my sixth-grade year of homeschooling with my mom. She was certified to teach only through sixth grade. Going back to PNG would mean sending me away to boarding school for seventh grade, so my parents decided to stay in the States.

We moved to a small ranching town in New Mexico and lived in a tiny, run-down trailer on my uncle's property. It was clustered near the trailers that my newly widowed grandmother and my uncle's family lived in. Although my father tried hard to find work in the town, there wasn't much to be found. He did whatever odd jobs he could, and my mother was hired by the local school to teach second grade.

In this new school, I learned to adapt to ruthlessness. I had learned to fit in and had gotten so good at the language in PNG that I sounded like a native. Now, however, in this small, cowboy town in rural New Mexico, I was lost. I went to school and immediately realized that I was the weird missionary kid who didn't fit in and whom everyone made fun of. Not that I didn't deserve it. I remember telling other kids when they would swear that they "shouldn't swear because Jesus wouldn't like that" and then getting punched in the stomach for saying it. Boy, was I clueless! I hadn't really developed physically yet either, so getting bullied by the bigger kids around me became a daily routine. I realized I'd have to adapt and get tough to survive. At the time, I had no idea how that early life lesson would help me in my business life, where ruthless survival would be taken to a whole new level.

NEVER GETTING AHEAD

After a year in New Mexico, we moved again, this time to Phoenix, Arizona. We always seemed to be broke, and I wondered what my parents were doing wrong and why we never had any money. My dad found a low-level accounting job, and my mom taught fifth grade at a Christian school, making a $12,000 salary per year. Thankfully, teachers' kids attended for free, or they never could have afforded to send me and my sister to a private school.

BREAKING RULES, WHETHER WE LIKED IT OR NOT

The Christian school I attended in Phoenix was very strict, with a rigid dress code and military-like expectations of conduct. At that time, having holes in your jeans was culturally considered "cool," but our school had clear rules against it. With our family's financial circumstances, rules like this were sometimes hard to follow.

After school one day, I was outside playing soccer with some friends and a slide tackle landed me with a gaping hole in my jeans—the only pair I owned. I had no choice but to wear the torn jeans to school again the next day.

I walked through the hallways feeling nervous, hoping no one would say anything. However, the principal saw me walk by and pulled me aside.

"Jonathan," he said, "why are you wearing jeans with a hole in the knee?"

"This is my only pair of pants," I said, embarrassed that it was true.

The principal assumed I was lying and became furious with me. He grabbed me sternly by the arm and marched me straight down to my mom's classroom and banged on the door.

"How can I help you, sir?" she said, looking nervous as she stepped out and closed the door behind her.

"I am sorry to disturb you, Mrs. Keyser," said the principal, "but I just caught Jonathan in a lie and wanted to make you aware of it. You know that holey jeans are not acceptable here, and Jonathan is telling me these are the only pair of pants that he has. I want you to be aware of his lie, and that I plan on an appropriate punishment."

Tears filled my mother's eyes as she told him that these *were* the only pair of jeans I had. She told him that my dad was out of work at the moment, and we couldn't afford to buy a new pair. She told the principal she would try to patch them that evening so I wouldn't break the rule anymore.

Needless to say, the principal felt horrible. He fumbled over his words as he backpedaled and apologized profusely to my mom. He said he would try to find me a pair of pants to wear and walked me sheepishly back to the school office. Rummaging through the lost-and-found pile, he found a pair of stonewashed jeans, which just happened to be my size, and gave them to me. Boy, was I excited as these were the coolest, in-style type of jeans at that time!

Boy, I felt good leaving the principal's office wearing these hip "new" jeans. Not only were they the first in-style jeans I had ever owned, but they also happened to fit me well for once. I was so excited to have cool new jeans—that weren't hand-me-downs or from a thrift store—that I wore them proudly every day until I outgrew them. My simple need had been filled through the school's lost and found, all because of a soccer game and a principal's mistake.

SO MUCH MORE

My parents continued to struggle financially. There were many times we weren't sure how we would be able to make the $700-per-month payment on our home. I can't tell you how many times my father called our family into the living room to pray intensely for a miracle. I remember many times praying fervently that we wouldn't get kicked out of our home.

Every time, we somehow made the payment. Sometimes people from the church would help us out; other times money would just show up from some completely unexpected source. It was amazing how our needs were always met, even when the situation looked hopeless.

Through all of this, my parents' care and compassion for others continued. They were constantly taking in people who needed a place to stay. Friends going through painful situations would call us, knowing that my parents would welcome them and help them through their difficult times.

I'll never forget my parents' decision to quasi-adopt two refugee girls into our family, one from Bosnia and the other from Afghanistan. They were not officially my sisters because they had families of their own—refugees from two different overseas wars—but they spent a lot of time in our home and became "honorary" members of our family. And they still are. My parents loved them and helped them all they could, even going so far as to pay the tuition for one of the girls to attend the school where my mom taught.

For my parents, it wasn't a question of whether they could afford to bring someone into our family—they just did.

CHAPTER 3

MORE THAN A PIZZA DELIVERY GUY

By the time I reached my junior year of high school, I was in public school—and I was thankful for that because I hated the legalism and strict rules of the Christian school I had been attending. I finally got to go to a "normal" school like other "normal" kids.

I'd finally started to make more friends, had a part-time job, and even had a girlfriend. Yet I had no vision for what I wanted to do beyond graduation. My parents had never brought it up, and I had honestly never thought about the future. So when my dad walked into my room one day and asked me what I wanted to do with my life, I was a bit dumbfounded.

"What do you mean?" I said. "I'm a pizza delivery guy. That's going really well. I am the top-earning driver in my store. I think I'll probably stick with that."

"I've been thinking about you," he said, "and I think you can do better." He reminded me of a conversation we'd had years ago in which he'd told me that I had a talent for arguing. "I think you should consider becoming a lawyer," he said.

I couldn't believe it. Me? A lawyer? *Wow.* It seemed impossible. I thought only big-time smart people could be lawyers, not a missionary kid, Domino's delivery driver like me! The whole idea seemed preposterous. I never would have pictured it. But that very day, for the first time in my life, I started thinking bigger than pizza. I figured I'd better go to college if I wanted to be a lawyer, and I'd better choose a good school so I could get a good job once I graduated.

I decided I wanted to chase the California dream, so I applied and somehow was accepted into UCLA, where I studied hard and made up for my previous unimpressive grade average. While taking a full course load and maintaining a straight-A average, I also had a job to pay my bills and somehow still managed to join a fraternity and have a social life.

Before starting at UCLA, I took a quarter off school to

establish residency and to work to save up some money for school. I ended up working at Domino's Pizza in a little California town named La Cañada, where I lived temporarily with a family that had taken me in. Unfortunately, the demand for pizza delivery there was much less than the store in Arizona that I had come from, so my plan to make and save up enough money for school wasn't going very well. As I swept the filthy pizza-shop floors one evening as we were closing up, a buddy of mine who was cleaning up with me suggested that I take a look at a new venture he was just getting into that supposedly gave you the ability to make up to $4,000–$5,000 per month.

That was a fortune to me at the time, so I was all ears. I followed his advice and ended up becoming an independent contractor for MCI on a special program to sign people up for MCI's long-distance service. Because I could speak some Spanish, I focused on the Hispanic community in Los Angeles, many of whom were paying exorbitant rates to call their families in Mexico. I went to where the people were. Because many in the Hispanic community in LA at the time paid their bills in person with cash, I would set up a card table on the sidewalk in front of the payment centers and help them switch to MCI. I worked extremely hard and eventually became the top guy nationally in this special program. Through this opportunity, I proved to myself that I could be successful, and my earnings helped me pay my way through school. My parents' selfless service had left them poor, and this was my first taste of financial success from hard work.

REDIRECTION

Then, at the end of my junior year as an undergraduate at UCLA, my favorite professor pulled me aside one day and told me he didn't believe becoming an attorney was the right path for me.

"What do you mean?" I asked, bewildered. "That's been my plan from day one! My political science major is preparing me for this, and I have worked very hard toward this goal!"

He said he didn't believe I'd enjoy a career in law. He felt my strengths lay in a different field and that I should look for a profession that was more entrepreneurial and people-oriented. I was somewhat surprised to hear this, as no one had ever told me that I was entrepreneurial or had decent people skills. I knew I had done well with delivering pizzas and with MCI, but I figured it was just because I worked harder than anyone else. My professor told me he believed I would be much happier in a different line of work, and I stumbled away from his office speechless and with my head spinning.

I wrestled with what to do. I had a lot of respect for that

professor and knew that he always had my best interests at heart. That conversation turned out to be another turning point in my life. Today, I am so grateful that he cared enough to tell me the truth. I would be miserable today as an attorney, and I would have missed out on the incredible journey that brought me to writing this book. Fortunately, I took his advice and decided to figure out what I wanted to do with my life.

Unsure of what to do next, I printed a bunch of résumés and went to a job fair at UCLA. I handed out over fifty résumés, one for every one of the companies in attendance, regardless of industry or job description. I received a bunch of letters from these companies in response, so many that it was overwhelming. I had no idea what any of these companies did and no real direction on which to pursue. I responded to a couple of big-name firms that I recognized, but within the first five minutes of each interview, it was clear that it would not be a good fit.

Frustrated, I pinned all the letters up on a corkboard in my room to deal with at a later time.

After a few days went by, my friend Jon came over and pulled an interest letter from a local commercial real estate brokerage firm off the corkboard. He handed the letter to me and said I should interview with them, stating, "You would be perfect for that job.

"Do you want your own private jet someday?" he asked.

"Umm...yes!" I said. "Of course I do."

"Well, then, this is your ticket."

The thought that I, a poor kid from Papua New Guinea, could own a private jet someday was preposterous to me!

Needless to say, I was sold. I called and scheduled an interview at the brokerage firm. From the moment I walked in, I loved everything about it. I loved the people I met there who all seemed highly driven, motivated, and focused on success. I saw guys in fancy suits driving nice cars and working in high-rise office buildings. They had pictures on their desks of their beautiful wives and families at exotic vacation destinations. They told me there was no income ceiling—that you could make as much money as you wanted as long as you worked really, really hard. Well, working hard was what I specialized in at that point, and after seeing all this, I had made my decision. This is what I wanted to do. I wanted in!

CHAPTER 4

A CHALLENGE TO CHANGE EVERYTHING

Wanting to make sure I started with the best possible brokerage firm, I pulled the list of the top commercial real estate brokerage firms and called the first five firms on the list. After interviewing heavily and receiving a number of offers, I decided to go with Grubb & Ellis.

I was on my way!

STARTING AT ZERO

The day I started at Grubb & Ellis, they basically tossed me a phone book and said, "Go make it happen." With zero experience or real estate knowledge, I became a business development machine for the company. That was what new brokers did. The firm paid you a tiny salary for one year and the rest was pure commission. If you could "make it happen" and generate and close enough deals, you might actually survive and be part of the 20 percent who "made it" in the business. They tracked how many phone calls and walk-in solicitations that we "newbies" made, and they gave out awards for the top cold-callers. I always made sure that was me. I wanted to be successful, and I wasn't going to let anyone or anything get in my way.

I had heard stories of dog-eat-dog behavior in commercial real estate brokerage, but I had no idea how ruthless and cutthroat the business actually was until I got started. I still remember Joe—a seasoned veteran broker with a frail figure and fierce, white hair who was years past retirement age—pulling me aside after my first few weeks and whispering to me, "Jonathan, you seem like a sweet kid. My one piece of advice for you is to watch your back. This industry is full of sharks, and every man is out for himself. Nice guys get trampled in this industry. You are going to need to look out for number one and play the game if you ever expect to survive in this crazy and vicious industry."

I took old Joe's words to heart. I had seen the example of my parents spending their lives serving others and being constantly broke, and I did not want that life. I wanted to be rich, and I wanted the success that these senior brokers around me had. If this is what it took to be successful, then I was in. Having already experienced the culture of ruthlessness in my first few weeks at the firm, I decided right then and there that I was going to be the most ruthless broker of them all. I wasn't going to let anyone take advantage of me. I was going to win at all costs.

And that is exactly what I did!

LYING WITH SINCERITY

I quickly learned a skill that "all successful brokers know" and that is how to lie very convincingly to someone's face while smiling and acting extraordinarily sincere and genuine. This is a skill you learned quickly. If you thought someone was close to guessing who your prospect or client was, you had to throw them off the trail... and fast!

In my first couple of months, I cold-called a company who needed to lease a new building for their growing operation. They agreed to let me help them find the right building. Similar to many real estate transactions, this client relationship was a verbal agreement and my tactic was to send them as many availabilities as possible and try to create urgency in the client's mind. I wanted them to sign a lease or purchase a building with me as fast as possible, before another broker caught wind and tried to steal the client out from under me.

Other brokers in the office overheard my phone conversations with this good-sized client, and suddenly, I had a bunch of newfound friends in the office stopping by my cube. Saying they were there just to "chat and catch up," their eyes frantically darted around my desk area looking for any signs of who the company was so they could call on them and offer to replace me. They would say things like, "Nice job, Jonathan, getting a live one! Tell me a little about what they need...I know a few off-market opportunities, and I may have an idea to help you. Where are they located now?"

Joe's advice rang in my ears as these new fake friends clambered around me, and I smiled and lied. I told them that it wasn't really a good opportunity, that it was actually much smaller than it sounded, and anything else I needed to say to discourage their interest. Just as soon as the new friends had come, they departed to seduce information out of the next young guy.

After realizing that some of the brokers were making deals with support staff to listen in on calls made in office conference rooms, I learned the importance of making significant client phone calls from my car. I also became very good at saying anything, regardless of truth, to get a client to sign a deal. Since brokers are compensated as a commissioned percentage of the total price, the longer the lease, the higher the rent, or steeper the sales price, the more commission the broker received. That was the game.

Almost all of the countless books I read on sales and success taught techniques to manipulate people in order to get what you wanted out of them. So that's exactly what I did. I'd show only the highest commission properties, leaving lesser paying properties off the list altogether. I became good at "creating false urgency" by telling clients, though it was rarely the case, that someone else wanted the space that they were interested in to imply the feeling of potential loss. I learned the widespread practice of "representing" both sides of real estate transactions to boost my commission and learned that I increased my chances further by going along with whatever the prospect or client said, even if it was wrong, racist, or unethical.

It wasn't unusual for me to bad-mouth or give negative information about another broker, true or otherwise, to get a potential client to sign with me. I wanted to win at all costs, and I truly believed at the time that this inauthentic and manipulative approach was what I needed to get ahead. The more it worked, the more I believed.

TURNING ON MY OWN KIND

I was also ruthless inside the office, doing exactly what I'd worked so hard to guard myself against. I would try to overhear other brokers' conversations with clients or inspect a fellow broker's desk for clues to active prospects that I could then pursue. I would even ask another broker in the office questions as if I were representing a new prospective client for their property. Then I would turn around and use that information to try to poach tenants from those same buildings and relocate them to a different building for my own benefit.

When I was working on a project with someone else in the office, I would try everything to take over the process and marginalize them so that at the end of the transaction, I would negotiate a higher percentage for myself. When we discussed commission splits, I would negotiate aggressively for the highest percentage possible, regardless of what the other person truly deserved or what was the fair or right thing to do.

PULLING ON STRINGS

In the community, if I ever "gave" anyone anything during this period in my life, it was always with strings attached. I would introduce a contact in the market to a potential client and expect them to return the favor immediately. If they didn't, I would complain that this individual was a "taker" and then warn the person that they needed to return the favor or I would cut them off.

With nothing but ruthless undermining and manipulation left in my wake, I had become a believer and master of this me-first philosophy.

But there was something wrong. I didn't like the person I was becoming. I began to wonder if I really had to be this ruthless to win. The road I was on was lonely and phony, and I was realizing that I wasn't where I wanted to be.

CHALLENGING THE NORM

To this day, all the big, traditional commercial real estate brokerage firms represent both landlords and tenants in lease negotiations. Even as a brand-new rookie, this approach didn't logically make sense to me. I never understood how anyone could represent opposing sides of a negotiation. In my mind, that would be like trying to represent both a husband and a wife in a divorce proceeding. How in the world could that be in the best interest of both clients? But it happened. Constantly. That was the name of the game: get both sides of the commission whenever possible.

Early on, I would ask senior brokers around me, "How can we tell tenants that we're getting them the best deal possible when, really, we're trying to steer them into a building that pays us the most commission and that our firm either represents or wants to represent?"

Each time, I was told, "No, no. We can effectively represent both sides. You are overthinking it. This is just how the business works and how it's been done for years. It's all about maximizing the commissions. Get back to work, rookie!" So I went to work trying to represent both sides of as many transactions as I could.

Then came a momentous meeting with the new CFO of one of our clients, and everything shifted for me.

This client's business was growing. They needed to negotiate a 100,000-square-foot lease to give the company the additional expansion space they needed. They had just hired a new CFO, and she called us into her office to determine whether we were the right fit to help them acquire their new space.

I became really excited when she began asking my senior broker the same kinds of questions that I had been asking, questions about our representing both sides of a transaction. She grilled us, asking how we could effectively represent tenants when we also represented a significant portion of the landlords in town who provided our firm with our majority share of revenue. I waited eagerly for my senior colleague to give a brilliant answer. But he didn't. He had no good response. We were fired on the spot by the new CFO, abruptly losing our client.

I was stunned. I *wasn't* an idiot. My questions *were not* dumb. There was something there!

That meeting quietly stirred something deep within me, planting a tiny seed of realization that ruthless and conflicted behavior doesn't always lead to success and that there might be a better way.

Yet even with that eye-opening experience, lying and backstabbing was the norm for me. Truth was not relevant. The *only* thing that mattered was this: whatever needed to be said or done to get a client and get a deal done so I could get paid is what I did. Period. Lying became so normal that I forgot I was even lying. I was just doing my job "being a broker," as all brokers do. I became numb to my actions and pushed the feelings of guilt deep down inside.

Like old Joe had said, I needed to be ruthless to win, and I became the most ruthless of them all. In my first year, I figured out how to lie, cheat, and steal all the way to Rookie of the Year. I was a success. My parents were proud, having no idea of what I was actually doing to be successful. I was finally making money, and my career was finally starting to take off.

CHAPTER 5

TRAPPED IN THE CRAZY COMMERCIAL REAL ESTATE BROKERAGE INDUSTRY

I thought it would be appropriate at this point to opine, for a minute, on the people in the commercial real estate industry so you, as the reader, don't get the impression that I am saying that they are all a bunch of scumbags. They're not, and truthfully, many of them feel trapped, as I once did.

I love the commercial real estate industry, and I love many of the people in it. It is one of the coolest industries out there. As a broker, there is no limit to your earning potential; you get pure market feedback based on whether you get hired or whether you can negotiate great deals for your clients, and it is filled with entrepreneurial, talented, and motivated individuals. Some of the nicest and most sincere people I have ever met are brokers, and many of them I consider lifelong friends.

As with other industries that are similarly ruthless and cutthroat, the problem is not the people. I believe that most people like me get into fields like commercial real estate brokerage because they want to be successful and they really want to help people. The problem is the system, and once people get in, they experience and truly believe that the only way to get ahead is to behave ruthlessly. They adapt and adjust and, over time, become merciless and predatorial individuals.

Think about the pressure—100-percent-commission environment, a finite number of companies in the market to represent, and zero compensation unless you win and close a deal. Add to that the fact that firms provide abundant praise and recognition for those who become "top producers." The pressure to perform causes people to behave in ways very different from how they would otherwise. Over time—just like the proverbial frog in the pot of water on the stove—as the temperature slowly increases, brokers adjust slowly, and before they know it, well-intentioned people have turned into ruthless sharks. By the time this happens, their lifestyle has adjusted to the income they are used to making and they feel trapped as I once did. They love the success and the money and the freedom that comes with brokerage, but they hate the culture of hypercompetitive, dog-eat-dog behavior. Like me, they simply don't see a way out.

I think many of you may be reading this right now thinking, "Hey, Jonathan is talking about me! My industry is ruthless just as he is describing." The problem is that very few people in ruthless businesses are proactively doing something to change this culture. Well, no one until me, which is why I am writing this book and why I am inviting you throughout to learn how to create success *without* having to behave in these uncharacteristic ways.

There is a better way.

I believe we can help thousands of brokers and other professionals get "untrapped" and find a healthier, happier way to win. So keep reading. Follow me on my journey just a bit further, and I'll open the door to bringing success through service to your own company and industry—whatever that may be.

CHAPTER 6

A DIRECTIONAL SHIFT

Some of you reading this were not yet active in business during the market crash that followed 9/11. Let me tell you, it was brutal. I still remember it like it was yesterday. Waking up to phone calls and emails to turn on my TV. I watched transfixed as the first tower fell and then drove into work to find the whole company standing around the TV watching the second tower fall. I didn't realize at the time how big of an effect it would have on my career, but it sure did.

Before that time, the dot-com boom was humming and people were throwing stupid money into startups of all kinds, particularly online businesses. By then, I had become a commercial real estate technology company specialist and *nearly* all of my clients were emerging technologies companies. When the dot-com bust hit in the early 2000s, over 95 percent of online startups went under, causing me to lose almost every client I had.

Then when 9/11 happened, everything changed. This was the first sizable domestic terrorist attack, and it created so much uncertainty and fear in the market overall that the real estate market came to a virtual standstill. To give you an idea of how dramatic it was, the year after 9/11, the amount of real estate activity in the Arizona real estate market dropped by 90 percent, and the remaining 10 percent of real estate activity that remained was much less lucrative. Many brokers retired, took sabbaticals, or changed industries altogether. Many of my friends who were overleveraged lost everything and had to start all over.

A TIME OF REEVALUATION

My business, like many brokers', evaporated overnight; that led to a very humbling bankruptcy, which I never thought I would have to go through. I was once again broke, and I learned the hard way the valuable lesson of client and industry diversification. Once again, I was in need.

Having no clients in a dead market gave me a unique opportunity to reevaluate my current situation. After interviewing with a number of firms, I decided to leave

Grubb & Ellis to take a risk and join a small, new commercial real estate firm in Phoenix. I was tired of working for a big firm, and at this new firm, I hoped to eventually become a partner and build some long-term value for myself versus just being a broker at a traditional firm. There, I started the painful process of slowly rebuilding my book of business.

After a couple of years, the market slowly started to improve again, and a nationwide network of independent firms approached us and asked our small, local firm to become their Phoenix affiliate office.

A NEW MODEL

Soon after, I attended an industry conference in Miami. As I looked through the breakout session topics, I saw one for networking and decided I wanted to learn more.

The breakout session leader talked about a different way of doing business that was intriguing. He spoke about a helping-others-first model, laying out a strategy I had not heard before. He explained the idea of developing long-term referral relationships and planting seeds through service that would end up producing rewards in the future. I was fascinated.

As the speaker finished his session, everyone else got up

and left the room, but I sat fixated in my chair. Mesmerized. Why was this the first I had heard of this approach, and why weren't more business leaders implementing it? As he packed up his stuff, I approached the speaker and asked, "This all sounds great, but does it really work? And if so, how do I actually do it?"

He said it did work, but that it took careful execution and a long-term vision, which was why very few people did it. He described it as the difference between planting trees and hunting. "If you plant citrus trees and nurture them, they take years to grow, but once they do, you have more fruit than you could ever eat. If you go hunting instead, you might get something right away, but you have to get up every day and do it all over again. This strategy I just described, Jonathan, is about building a network of people who want to help you because you have spent so much time helping them."

My head spun. I had never heard anything like this before. His words sounded vaguely familiar, echoing the ways my parents had raised me, but it made no sense. Why were my parents broke but this guy was super-successful if they both practiced helping others? I was skeptical and intrigued, and I needed to learn more. If I could actually create the same or better level of success without having to be the ruthless prick that I had become, I had to learn how.

I asked if there was anyone else I could speak with about it, and he gave me the name of one other individual who was doing a version of what he described. Before he walked out, he reiterated to me very clearly that this was a long-term strategy and that doing it would not be easy. But in the long run, his opinion was that the upside was worth it.

That was it. I had to track down this other guy and find out if this new way of doing business could really work.

CHAPTER 7

THE MAKING OF A MAVERICK

I tracked the guy down that the conference session leader had told me to speak with, who turned out to be a very caring and service-minded individual. He was gracious enough to let me follow him around for half a day as I peppered him with questions. The things he shared with me were so simple and so basic. It was the same stuff my parents had taught me growing up, which both confused and intrigued me. He had just figured out how to make money doing it. I was blown away. I realized that he was truly a maverick, and I wanted to be a maverick like him.

He handed me a copy of *Never Eat Alone* by Keith Ferrazzi, a book he said was the best he ever read on the subject.

THE ROAD MAP TO BROKE (AGAIN)

"This is your road map," he said. "Make sure to read it cover to cover. There's more in here than you could ever get from a single meeting with anyone."

I asked him why, if this strategy of helping others created such success for the giver, there were not more business people doing it? His answer mirrored what the breakout session leader had told me. He said, "Jonathan, the reason why no one does this is because it takes too long, and you have to go against the grain and culture of the industry you are in. People don't want to be different. They want to fit in. If you implement this strategy, it will take years to create success and most people don't want to do that. They want instant gratification and the shortest path to success, but what they don't realize is that they are sacrificing long-term, sustainable success for short-term gain."

I sat quietly scribbling notes and processing this new information. "To do this, Jonathan, you have to start all over," he said. "Financially, it will be like going back to being a rookie again for at least four years, maybe five, before you start making any kind of real money again—and that's if you work at this relentlessly. You will be literally starting over."

He continued to make sure I understood how hard this

would be. "People will criticize and question you, and it's going to be frustrating and hard. But if you stick with it and don't give up, you will eventually start reaping the benefits."

I took a breath, looked him in the eye, and said, "I have been broke many times in my life, and I am not afraid of being broke again. If this really is possible, I want to do it because I am sick and tired of this ruthless industry and how I feel I have to act to be successful. I will do the plan as you have laid it out. I won't quit, and I will make it successful in Arizona."

He looked at me and nodded knowingly with the air of someone who had heard similar words before. I don't think he realized at the time how serious I was.

MOTIVATED TO CHANGE COURSE

On the plane back to Arizona, his words just kept racing around and around in my head. Could I, a missionary kid turned ruthless broker from Phoenix, Arizona, actually do this and be successful? Did I have what it took? Could I do this in Arizona in commercial real estate without becoming homeless?

I wrote down everything I could remember from the meeting. My attempts at sleep that night were impossible. I felt different, excited, motivated...and scared.

This philosophy was vastly different from what I had been trained to do. This was in many respects the polar opposite of everything I had done in commercial real estate to date. Rather than cold-calling and selling, I was now supposed to get involved in the community and see how many people I could help? It sounded crazy, yet deep inside, there was a quiet realization that this was what I had been looking for. I realized that if I could create success this way, I would never have to be the "old me" again.

I realized, as well, that I now had to go through the painful process of unlearning most of the bad habits I had accumulated if I was ever going to be successful through this new strategy. As scared as I was, I was up to the task, and I went to work reinventing myself.

CHAPTER 8

CONNECTING THROUGH HELPING

I read Keith Ferrazzi's amazing book, *Never Eat Alone*, cover to cover—twice—and started down the path laid out for me. I understood that everything about my old business plan—playing both sides of the deal, scratching and clawing for everything I could get, talking people into deals that weren't good for them, building a wall of protection around myself—would have to go out the window. I had to abandon the traditional commercial real estate brokerage sales model—targeting companies, pursuing them relentlessly until they succumbed to the pressure and finally agreed to hire us.

The advice I'd been given was a gift that I now pass on to you. He told me that the best way to make connections that lead to business is this: *help people with whatever they need.*

His simple way of establishing long-term, sustainable client relationships completely changed the way I thought. My eyes were now opened to a new world of opportunity, and I was excited.

STARTING AT THE BOTTOM...AGAIN

I had no high-level business connections or contacts when I started. Unlike others who grew up in country clubs and went to the elite prep schools with other rich kids, I had no one. No super-connected or rich old roommates, teammates, or country club buddies to send business or connections my way. At first, I looked at this as a disadvantage, but as time went on, this lack of connectivity turned out to be an advantage. I had the opportunity to create fresh first impressions with people in the marketplace.

Rather than chasing companies and constantly trying to sell myself, I got involved in the community with a focus on helping everyone that I could. I determined that I would never again walk away from any significant interaction with anyone without finding three or more meaningful ways to help them.

This was new territory for me.

I booked thousands of coffees, lunches, drinks, and dinners. I sat down with people and listened to their stories. I spent countless hours with both profit and nonprofit business organizations to help raise money, increase membership, and raise their profiles within their respective communities.

Another choice I made was to focus on identifying and serving people who were more successful than I, people who were well-connected in the business community. In serving them, I kept hearing about the power of perseverance. Many successful people told me that the key to their success was not intelligence or talent but rather their habit of never giving up. "It is all about mindset," they would say. "Persistence, getting up in the morning, doing the little things, and doing them relentlessly until they are done." I learned that truly successful people never say, "I might." They always say, "I will or I won't. No gray area." Unsuccessful people say, "I think I'll try" about any number of ideas, and then they bounce around, not sticking with anything.

The bottom line was clear: work harder than anyone else, and never quit.

Drawing on the experience of others was invaluable. Every meeting was a gift. I was able to develop a strong network of business people and friends, which included a host of new contacts among the giants in the business. Today, this is one of my biggest assets, and they're ready to be yours, too, laid out as simple strategies for you to follow in the chapters ahead.

CHAPTER 9

THE WORK THAT LED TO BALANCE

I was relentless in my efforts. Morning, noon, and night, I worked the plan that I had committed to. Just as predicted, the work was not reflected in my bank account. Years passed, and nearly everyone lost faith in the system I had embraced. They lost faith in me.

The questions that pushed against my commitment to selfless service came pouring in from all sides. "What are you doing, Jonathan?" they asked. "You're going into debt. You're in trouble financially. This new idea, whatever it is, is not good for you or your business."

I would shake my head and press on. Even on days when I was frustrated, even on days when I wanted to agree with

THE WORK THAT LED TO BALANCE · 77

them, I'd say, "I'm going to try it for a little bit longer." Sometimes I honestly didn't know why I kept at it.

Many smart and successful business people continued to scoff and mock me when I told them about my vision. They would say how unrealistic I was. "The world really doesn't work like that, Jonathan," they said. "It's a dog-eat-dog industry you are in. You have to play the game. You are naive and idealistic. You need to come back to reality."

"If you don't watch out for yourself, no one will," others would say. "You would do better to focus on selling and getting revenue rather than running around trying to help others succeed all the time."

Many people told me I was being irresponsible. Even my wife at the time would openly question how I could work so hard and still not have the success that I used to have and that my peers were experiencing. I never spent time selling, but rather I was spending all my waking hours doing a bunch of things for others that looked like non-profit work or community service. As time went on and without much personal revenue coming in, this started to look more and more like a very flawed strategy.

NAYSAYERS ARE RARELY RIGHT

Frankly, I don't blame my critics. On the surface, they certainly appeared to be correct and genuinely concerned. In hindsight, I don't know how I was able to survive and continue working the plan through all the negativity and criticism. But I refused to quit, because deep inside me I felt like it would work...eventually.

I continued to remind myself that most people quit right on the verge of success. I could feel that what I was building would pay off in the long run, so the setbacks didn't matter. I reminded myself that I was not going to be one of the people who quit. I was going to be one of the guys who made it, and I was going to do it through selflessness. At my lowest point, I looked in the mirror and made a commitment to myself. I determined that I would keep pushing ahead and make this work—or die trying. I was going to prove them wrong. Yes, I had doubts, and I had loads of worries, but I brushed them aside, put my head down, and worked harder than ever.

As a child, I memorized a poem that has come to my mind many times in my life and in the building of our extraordinary, mission-driven business:

IT COULDN'T BE DONE

BY EDGAR ALBERT GUEST

Somebody said that it couldn't be done

But he with a chuckle replied

That "maybe it couldn't" but he would be one

Who wouldn't say so till he'd tried.

So he buckled right in with the trace of a grin

On his face. If he worried he hid it.

He started to sing as he tackled the thing

That couldn't be done, and he did it!

Somebody scoffed: "Oh, you'll never do that;

At least no one ever has done it;"

But he took off his coat and he took off his hat

And the first thing we knew he'd begun it.

With a lift of his chin and a bit of a grin,

Without any doubting or quiddit,

He started to sing as he tackled the thing

That couldn't be done, and he did it.

There are thousands to tell you it cannot be done,

There are thousands to prophesy failure,

There are thousands to point out to you one by one,

The dangers that wait to assail you.

But just buckle in with a bit of a grin,

Just take off your coat and go to it;

Just start to sing as you tackle the thing

That "cannot be done," and you'll do it.

POETRY FOUNDATION

CHAPTER 10

A BOOK AND A COACH

Reading *Never Eat Alone* had given me the road map to creating a network based on service. I knew I had a lot more to learn, though, so I filled my nights and car rides reading and listening to books.

As an avid reader since childhood, I had read piles of self-help, sales, wealth, and personal power material over the years. I learned a lot from my reading, but much of it always felt a little off, though at the time, I couldn't put my finger on why.

A BOOK CAN LEAD TO MORE

One day, a friend of mine in the business community recommended that I read *17 Lies That Are Holding You Back and the Truth That Will Set You Free* by Steve Chandler.

I'd read many books, and I thought this was just another one of them.

I was wrong. This book was different.

In the book, Steve laid out seventeen common lies that we believe about ourselves that keep us from being everything that we are capable of. As I read this book, I realized that I believed many of the lies myself. I realized that part of why it was taking so long to create success with this new service model was that I had a head full of false beliefs and negative self-talk. I realized in a flash that I was inadvertently creating barriers to my own success in my own mind. This rocked me to my core. As I read, I came to understand that I already had all of the power I needed to free myself from these self-limiting beliefs and transform my life through a different way of *being*. I just didn't know how to do it!

Page after page, chapter after chapter, I could not put Steve's book down, finishing it in one night. The message fueled me. I immediately wanted to reread it, starting again on page one. I was fired up, filled with adrenaline. There was no way I could sleep. I opened my email and immediately typed a message to the author. I had never written an email to an author before, but I was so compelled by his book that I had to contact him.

"This is exactly the kind of stuff I've been looking for," I wrote. "I feel like I've been waiting my whole life for this book!" I knew this guy really understood. I wanted more. The book ended, but I needed to know how to take the newfound realizations and put them into practice. I had a lot more learning to do.

"I want you to coach me," I wrote, feeling bold even as I wrote the words. I had learned from my cursory online research that Steve was a famous author and successful life coach. I had glimpsed his genius and felt he was the one I needed to work with to help me change my thinking from fear and scarcity to abundance. I knew that there was still a long and difficult journey ahead, and I was sure I could not do this alone.

Humbling myself to ask for help was not easy. At this point in my life, I had never hired a coach or counselor. I had been so focused on safeguarding the perception of having it all together that hiring someone to tell me what to do was not an option. As my friends knew, I didn't like advice, even when it was *free*! But reaching out was one of the best decisions I have ever made.

I anxiously checked my email again and again over the next couple of days, waiting for Steve's response. When his reply finally came, I clicked it open excitedly. It was short and disappointing, stating that unfortunately, he wasn't coaching anymore but said he was speaking near me the following week and invited me to attend. I was disappointed, but I refused to accept his answer. I felt that he had the ability to help me transform my thinking and I wanted his help, and I was not going to give up so easily. I was set on working with Steve.

I accepted his invitation to attend his talk, determined that I would approach him and convince him to coach me after he finished his presentation. I attended his seminar, while clutching a copy of *17 Lies* like a favorite childhood toy. It was an excitement I had never before experienced.

His speech was amazing. He described the difference between an ownership mindset and a victim mindset, and I realized that I was the ultimate victim and constantly looked for excuses or reasons outside of myself for why things went wrong with my life. I saw that all of my unhappiness and pain came from thoughts that I believed about myself and the world outside of me. I saw a possibility for a different future if I changed my mindset.

After his speech, I was completely jazzed. His words had increased my desire to work with him even more. I lingered after the presentation, waiting for the line to speak with him to die down so that I could get my chance. Finally, it was just him and me.

Approaching him, I nervously said, "Hi, I'm Jonathan

Keyser. I wrote you an email a few days ago asking if you could coach me."

Steve shook his head. "Nice to meet you! I'm so glad you made it out here today, but as I told you, I just don't do that anymore. I'm sorry."

"Mr. Chandler," I said, speaking swiftly so he wouldn't have the chance to cut me off, "I promise that if you take me on, I will be a hundred percent coachable. I will soak up everything you give me like a sponge and put it into action in my life immediately." I continued, "You see, Mr. Chandler, I realized reading your book and listening to your talk that I keep thinking the answers to my problems are *outside* of me. You are the first person I have ever met who explained what I need to change *inside* of myself in a way that I could understand it. I am trying to be successful in commercial real estate brokerage by just helping other people, and I realize after reading your book that my own beliefs and mindset are completely off. You have something that I want; would you please reconsider and coach me?"

Steve sighed and looked around the room. Then he looked back at me. There was a light in his eyes. How could you say no to such a heartfelt appeal? To my delight, he reluctantly agreed to coach me for one year, with the condition that if I was not coachable at any moment and did not live up to our agreement, he would fire me on the spot.

Needless to say, I was pumped!

COACHABLE AND PRESENT

Steve Chandler's coaching over the next year was transformative in many ways. He taught me so much that I had never learned before about the power of the mind, the power of thought, the holding of a clear mental picture of what you wanted to create in life and living into it. I felt like I was in grade school again learning Arithmetic 101. I asked him many times during our coaching, "Why have I never learned this? It is all so simple and straightforward. How was I never taught this before by anyone?"

He taught me about the power of being fully present, about thinking really big. He taught me to not worry about what others think (versus pretending not to worry what others think), and about being bold and asking for exactly what I wanted out of life. Most importantly, he taught me about believing steadfastly in my own ability to create whatever I wanted in my own life. It was invaluable coaching, and it built the groundwork for what was to come. I had come so far in the year working with Steve. Little did I know at the time that working with Steve was only the beginning of my journey.

CHAPTER 11

THROUGH GREEN-COLORED GLASSES

"Green," I said, still thinking this was some kind of trick.

"So," supercoach Steve Hardison continued, "if you are wearing glasses with green lenses, no matter where you look, you see green. The problem is, you don't realize you're wearing glasses, so you don't know that the world is actually not green but a myriad of different colors that you don't even know exist. My promise to you, Jonathan, is that if you work with me, not only will I help you take those glasses off to see the world as it truly is, but I will actually introduce you to *yourself* for the very first time."

Steve Hardison had clearly seen through me on our very first meeting. On my drive home, I began to freak out, trembling so hard I could barely drive. I couldn't believe what had just happened. I felt exposed and uncomfortable. No one had ever gotten to me like that before. Ever.

Steve Chandler had told me after a couple of years of coaching that he would no longer work with me—he said I had been a great student but that he had taught me all that he could. I was so bummed. I wasn't done. I had so much more to learn! He told me that he felt I was ready to work with Steve Hardison, a supercoach I had heard about many times in our coaching sessions and had read about in Steve's books, but whom I had never met.

"Steve is the guy you want to work with," Steve said. "That is, if you're serious about this. If you really want to take your transformation to the next level."

Although I had never met him, I had heard that Steve Hardison was one of the most honest, intuitive, loving, and intense people you could ever meet. People described their first visits with him as amazing, yet terrifying. They say you can't hide anything from him, and he can see right through you. So, as you can guess, I was extremely nervous about meeting him despite my strong desire to do so. I was afraid that he would take one look at me and see what a regular person I was—so unworthy of working with a supercoach for top business leaders. Fueled by anxiety about the potentially unnerving experience of meeting with him, I procrastinated month after month and found endless reasons not to contact him.

MEETING HARDISON

A few months later, after a particularly frustrating few weeks at work, I mustered up the courage to call Steve and tell him that I was ready to contact Steve Hardison and asked him to set up an introduction.

When the day came to meet with Steve Hardison, I was nervous and jittery as I drove to his home; I had no idea what I would say when I got there. I got lost and was forty minutes late, which added to my stress as I had heard he was adamant about people being on time. I called and, with a timid voice, let him know I was running late. He was very gracious and warm in his response and assured me it was no problem. He then proceeded to give me verbal directions.

I finally arrived at his home in Mesa, Arizona—which was significantly more modest than the Beverly Hills-style compound I had expected—and I knocked softly on his front door. After a few seconds, the door flung open. I took one look at him and could hardly believe that the man standing before me was the real Steve Hardison. I had envisioned a muscular giant of a man, but instead I was greeted by a tall man with a regular build, soft voice, glasses, and a big, warm smile. He didn't seem like the kind who would slam you against a wall and force you to change your entire life.

His wife, Amy, was sweet and kind, bringing me tea and chatting with me like this was any other afternoon. The two of them weren't intimidating in the least but very loving and gentle. I started to relax, and Steve invited me to join him in his office.

And that is when everything changed.

A DIFFERENT WORLD

We walked into Hardison's office, which was a plush, well-decorated *casita* attached to his home, and he closed the door.

Without any warning, right before my eyes, a whole new person emerged! Steve Hardison started speaking, and suddenly the most intense yet loving person sat before me. I had never before been in the presence of anyone like that in my life. I felt like I was naked in the room, by the way he was talking and by what he was saying. I felt like he could see straight through me, under my skin, even into my heart.

Sitting there on the couch in Steve Hardison's office that afternoon, I felt vulnerable and unprotected, as if all of my fears, insecurities, and faults were out in the open. For the first time, I felt the terrifying feeling of being completely exposed and unable to get away. I squirmed in my chair and wished I could run away.

I can't remember everything that happened during the meeting, just the general feeling that I was being taken apart and laid out on the table for my own viewing. It was one of the most unnerving meetings of my life. The meeting was three and a half hours long, but it felt like three lifetimes.

I stumbled out of his office, got into my car, and drove away trying to process everything. I couldn't believe what had just happened to me. I had spent so much of my life hiding who I really was. I had never had someone see through me like that before. Ever.

TIME TO TAKE OFF THE GLASSES

At the time—after he had given me the metaphoric green-colored glasses to look through—I thought, "Wow, what a manipulative, brilliant thing to say. This guy is a salesman!" But deep down, I knew it was more than that. This wasn't a sales pitch at all. As hard as it was to fathom, this was the simple truth—the green-colored glasses had to come off.

CHAPTER 12

RECOGNIZING THE TRUTH

As the discomfort from my initial meeting with Steve Hardison slowly faded, I began to realize that I wanted what I believed he could teach me more than I feared the discomfort and vulnerability of working with him.

You see, the service model that I had now been pioneering was finally starting to generate business for me as people started referring clients to me. It was awesome. I didn't have to sell; I didn't have to put a PowerPoint together. I would just answer the phone, and a friend whom I had done something for previously would say, "Hey, Jonathan, thanks so much for helping me out with the connections you made for me a couple of years back. That was so kind and thoughtful. Question for you: Would you be interested in helping my company with their real estate needs? We need new office space, and I so appreciate all you did for me that I would love to return the favor by hiring you to represent us. You interested?"

SEEING THE SHIFT

It felt amazing that after so many years of struggle, I was finally starting to see results from my acts of service in the community. That said, I still felt incredibly empty inside, as if I was still missing a big part of life's puzzle on creating an extraordinary, happy, and successful life. I saw so many successful business people around me with miserable personal lives, using booze, drugs, or hobbies to push down the empty, unhappy feelings inside.

I felt as though I was learning in layers. As though I was peeling back the onion, seeing more and more things to make my life better, but that there were still a number of very important pieces missing. *Never Eat Alone* had taught me about relationship building and a new way of business through service. Steve Chandler had laid an incredible foundation, teaching me about mindset and the power of the mind. What I still lacked was knowing *how* to actually transform my mind.

I swallowed my fear, called Hardison, and thankfully, he agreed to take me on as a client. As I worked with him, my fear and discomfort faded, and I started to get a glimpse of what was still in the way of me truly excelling in this new service approach to life and business. Although I had been faithfully executing my business plan, serving others day in and day out, it was not bringing me the joy or fulfillment that I wanted. While I was finally making some money from my efforts, it was nowhere near top producer level, and I couldn't figure out why. My endless acts of service to others were actually wearing me down, and with Hardison's help, I was starting to realize why!

FALSE SELFLESSNESS

What I started to see more and more clearly as I worked with Hardison was that the problem lay not in my actions but rather in my motives. I was surprised to discover that despite my years of service to others in the community, I had actually not been operating from a true heart of service—as I had thought. My "good deeds" were actually coming from selfish motives.

Through service, I had unwittingly been promoting *myself*, keeping track of who I was helping in my mind and expecting them to reciprocate, and painting myself as this selfless guy in the community to make me seem like a good guy rather than just to help them. I realized I was using acts of service manipulatively as a sales technique rather than from a true place of wanting to help others. The crazy part is that I had been completely unaware of this until Hardison helped me see it. It was a very sobering realization.

Seeing how full of crap I had been was a hard pill to swallow. I had been lying to myself for so long that I actually thought I had developed a heart of service. But when I finally faced the truth head-on, I saw that my motives had been exactly the opposite of what I thought they were.

NEW VISION

I could finally see myself for who I had been: inauthentic, manipulative, and inherently selfish. I made the decision right then to throw myself 100 percent into the service of others. No longer would I keep track in my mind of whom I had helped, expecting it to come back to me. I would just let go and serve everyone from a pure place of love and service, trusting that the universe would at some point bring it back to me in the form of success.

I felt a new happiness surging within me that I had never felt before. I was no longer living a lie. I had taken the glasses off. I wasn't seeing green anymore!

I had a new ability to empathize and understand people's feelings after this breakthrough in a way I had never done before. I had a new appreciation for my children, for my family, for my childhood and the struggles we faced for so many years, and for my parents. I could see with new eyes, and I was filled with a deep sense of awe and appreciation for the world and everything in it. I felt deep love for all people, something I had certainly never completely experienced before. I finally understood what my parents had modeled for so many years. I could finally see clearly.

I also started to realize that Hardison was preparing me for something much bigger than I had ever imagined. During one of our sessions, he looked at me and said, "What if you had your own firm? What if you had even just four or five people who believed in what you were doing? What would that look like?"

I was stunned. "That's impossible!" I said. "Where am I going to find five people who want to work this way? I doubt myself half of the time."

He just smiled and repeated, "What if...?"

CHAPTER 13

THE GENUINE ME

No longer blinded by selfish ambition, I made the decision to serve, serve, and continue to serve—not worrying whether anyone helped me in return. I wanted to serve others just for the joy and honor it gave me of selflessly helping others, and the repercussions were profound.

I began having authentic conversations with people, not realizing up to that point that I had been so busy thinking about myself, I wasn't paying attention to them. I began to notice that other people's views of me and interactions with me improved significantly. I began to value each individual and to become committed to their success— for their own good this time, not mine.

This was the point where my success really started to take off. The stops were pulled out, and my personal book of business grew rapidly. People I served selflessly continued to show their appreciation by sending referrals, and those referrals turned into more and more clients.

A NEW DREAM

I was finally having significant financial success through the service model, but now I had a different problem. It became more and more obvious that the way I was doing business was simply too disruptive for the commercial real estate firm I was then working for. As I grew from mediocre producer to top producer in the office, there was a very clear disconnect between my team's method of doing business and the traditional modus operandi of others working around me.

It became more and more apparent that my new way of getting and serving clients would truly benefit from having a life of its own. I needed the ability to scale outside the limitations of a traditional firm.

Hardison's words kept ringing in my ears. I wondered what kind of results could be obtained if an entire company embraced such a way of doing business. By this point, I had received so many referrals from people I had served over the years that I thought about whether this could be effectively scaled and duplicated and taught successfully to others.

What if a whole company were built on selfless service? Was this an achievable dream? Just the thought was a bit intimidating. I'd had enough difficulty creating this new business model for myself and my small team. Would it be possible to perform the same feat with an entire company of people who were all dedicated and committed to this model? Was it possible to create a commercial real estate brokerage firm whose core foundational principle was loving and helping others?

These seemed like crazy thoughts, but the question continued to dance within me. And I wrestled with it inside myself for months.

One day, I decided to take a trip to Sedona, Arizona. Early that first morning, as I sat in a swirling hot tub staring in awe at the majestic mountains with a light snowfall falling on my head, I quieted my mind so I could relax and meditate. As I thought about Hardison's words, the thought hit me: "I am thinking *way* too small!" This business model I had stumbled across and pioneered in commercial real estate in Arizona had the potential to be bigger and far more powerful than I had yet comprehended. I saw an opportunity to change the entire real estate industry by proving one didn't have to be ruthless to be successful.

I suddenly recognized that all of the events of my entire

life, all the painful experiences, had perfectly prepared me for this moment. I decided right then and there to put my insecurities and fears aside and boldly launch my own firm with the dream of reimagining and reinventing the commercial real estate brokerage industry through selfless service. My head spun with this new awareness, and I felt a powerful surge of boldness. I could see clearly now what I needed to do. Finally!

CREATING A CULTURE

Grabbing my tablet off the chair next to the hot tub, I opened a new document and began to write down all the things I hated about the commercial real estate industry. Getting all of that out of my system, I then wrote down all the cultural things I wished were true in commercial real estate brokerage firms.

That wish list became the foundation that our founding team at Keyser built our 15 Core Operating Principles upon. Having a blank slate to work with, we fearlessly dared to imagine a reality that checked all of the boxes of a utopian commercial real estate company culture.

I resigned my position at my old firm and set out to create a company that would become the model for what self-less service in business looked like. Two members of my former firm and my assistant decided to join me to launch this new firm, and three of Hardison's children joined me as well.

We hired a professional branding firm to really help us hone our message; we spent hours and hours at coffee shops hovered over the operating principles that were in development. We discussed and debated and finally ended up with 15 Core Operating Principles that we all felt represented the culture we wanted to create.

BUILDING OUR COMPANY

I self-funded the company from my personal savings that had now built up over a few years of success. As funny as this seems now, I had planned for all of us to conduct business out of a coffee shop in the beginning because I needed to preserve capital, and I wasn't sure I could afford office space. Fortunately, an architectural firm we were friends with had extra cube space in the back of their office and generously offered to let us use it until we could afford our own space.

We spent hours pouring our hearts and souls into the company logo, messaging, and website, determined to ensure that the culture we sought to create would be reflected in our materials. Not only did we not care whether other firms would make fun of us for our message of love and service in commercial real estate, but we actually decided we would wear it as a badge of honor if they did because that meant that we were effectively communicating how different we really were.

THE LAUNCH

At last, Keyser officially opened for business on January 2, 2013, with seven founding members: Darius, Ian, Blake, Clint, Rae, and Lindsey, who were the first brave souls to take the risk, and me. This was an extraordinarily fun time. We were one tight-knit team. We worked crazy hard, we laughed together, we played together, and we made a commitment to just have fun and enjoy the journey we were on. We knew some people thought we were foolish, and we didn't care. We had a vision for the future, and no one was going to stop or discourage us from our goal.

One of the most surprising things when we launched the firm was that I thought 80 percent of people would not really understand what we were doing and simply discount us as crazy. As I said earlier, we were fine with that. We did not set out to appeal to the masses. We wanted to appeal to those who wanted to do business differently, with someone they trusted, who had integrity and would do the right thing by them at all times.

We actually found the opposite to be true. We had been so bold and fearless to clearly state our mission to transform the commercial real estate industry that most people embraced us, supported us, and went out of their way to try to help us succeed. This was one of the most unexpected and amazing parts of implementing our company's mission. People came out of the woodwork telling me stuff like:

"About time! We always wondered when you would start your own firm."

"Jonathan, I always knew you had it in you! Proud of you."

Each time, I was humbled and surprised because I had never known it was in me or thought it possible. But by deciding to take this bold step, the community rallied around us, and our growth and success has been nothing short of unbelievable since. The business was launched, and the immediate growth and reception we received confirmed our sense that this disruptive business model was definitely going to fill a big vacuum in our industry. We were off to a great start.

WHAT SELFLESS SERVICE PRODUCED

As this book publishes, Keyser has rapidly grown into the largest commercial real estate brokerage firm of our kind in the State of Arizona and one of the fastest growing in the United States. We are launching offices around the country and serve thousands of clients, helping them with their real estate needs all around the world. We have started a human capital consulting firm, helping other organizations train their people to operate at maximum potential. We have also just launched the Keyser Institute to train and certify individuals and organizations to create cultures that replicate The Keyser Experience in their own organizations. We call it The Keyser Way.

Today, the mission of Keyser has expanded beyond commercial real estate. Our mission is to change the business world through selfless service. Our strategy is to demonstrate that you truly can have extraordinary success by helping others succeed. We built a model to be intentionally easy to replicate by others, and already, we have seen other organizations across the globe implementing this strategy for themselves.

So how did we build a firm on the principle of selfless service, and how can you build or reinvent your own organization around the same principles?

Step into Part Two and keep reading!

PART / TWO

CREATING THE KEYSER EXPERIENCE FOR YOURSELF

A Master in the art of living draws no sharp
distinction between his work and his play,
his labor and his leisure,
his mind and his body,
his education and his recreation,
his love and his religion.
He hardly knows which is which.
He simply pursues his vision of excellence
through whatever he is doing,
leaving others to determine
whether he is working or playing.
To himself, he always appears to be doing both.

—LAWRENCE PEARSALL JACKS

The story of my journey in Part One serves multiple purposes. For me, it has brought me to this point in my life, here and now, that allows me to share my struggles and successes. For you, it has given you the opportunity to see the world and a self-destructive industry through the eyes of someone who believes it doesn't have to be that way. For all who want to change the culture of business, my story provides a launching point for disrupting industries around the world for the better.

There are times in life when we think, "It would've been much easier if I had learned this the first time around." I know because I felt the same way. But without our experiences, both the good and the bad, we would have missed out on the gift the journey has given us. The gift my journey has given me is the opportunity to gladly share the powerful difference selfless service can make in your life and business, as it has in mine.

The goal of Part One was for you, the reader, to understand my path to this new way of doing business and to give you a "behind-the-scenes look" so that you could understand for yourself how someone else actually created success for himself and for others utilizing this philosophy.

Now, moving forward to Part Two, we'll dig into the specifics of the Three Levels of Reinvention we used in creating The Keyser Experience we function on today. By sharing this process with you, you'll be able to create, or perhaps in your case re-create, a business model with which you can find success and have an extraordinary Keyser Experience while doing so. Not only do we utilize this three-step process within Keyser, but we also train executives across the globe how to reinvent themselves and their organizations using these three steps.

My goal for Part Two of my book is to take everything I have learned and condense it into the following chapters to give you everything you need to know to create a Keyser Experience for your own organization.

The Three Levels of Reinvention is a reinvention from the

inside out, which I believe is the only effective way to truly achieve success through service. The three levels are:

- Reinventing *yourself through selfless service.*

  "You must be the change you wish to see in the world."
  —MAHATMA GANDHI

- Reinventing *your company culture through selfless service.*

  "A star wants to see himself rise to the top. A leader wants to see those around him rise to the top."
  —SIMON SINEK

- Reinventing your approach to *your clients and collaborators*—through selfless service. Collaborators to us include your vendors, suppliers, influencers, partners, investors, and the business community as a whole.

  "He who wishes to secure the good of others has already secured his own."
  —CONFUCIUS

While simple on the surface, Keyser's three-level transformation process is profound in its application. It is truly a reinvention from the inside out, focusing on transforming yourself, the culture of your organization, and how you interact with your clients and partners. Without all three of these elements, your transformation will be incomplete and your success adopting this methodology will be limited at best. Reinvention around each of these three elements is key to the successful creation of The Keyser Experience within your organization.

Throughout Part Two, you'll also find the Keyser symbol placed in the inside margins by various paragraphs. On my book website, I have created a vault with information just for you. This symbol indicates additional resources and materials available to you on the specific topic at www.ruthlessbook.com/vault; it's there as a service to help you on your journey.

So how does one create transformation using this three-level process? As mentioned in Part One, we have built Keyser around 15 Core Operating Principles that are the backbone of everything we do. In the following chapters, I will discuss why they each matter, describe how we actually put these Principles into practice, and give very specific real-world examples. Like the three levels, these 15 Core Operating Principles seem simplistic on the surface, but together, they form a culture of service that can create extraordinary success in any organization. Throughout Part Two, you will have the benefit of hearing about my team's trials and errors and the lessons and tips we discovered on our journey so you can learn from our successes and avoid our mistakes.

Keyser's 15 Core Principles e-booklet is deliverable #1 for you and can be found at: www.ruthlessbook.com/vault.

Read carefully, and use your highlighter freely. I recommend reading sections twice when you find information that speaks directly to you and to your desire to be best-in-class in your industry. Meditate on the content, implement each strategy and tactic, and allow each one to have an impact. The simplicity of these Principles is what makes them so profound, as they are each based on the foundational value of being genuinely selfless in every action and interaction.

Within each of the fifteen Principles, we will highlight each of the three levels so you can see how each of the Principles embeds the three-level process within them. By the end, I believe you will start to see how each of these fifteen Principles tie together beautifully to create a culture and experience that is second to none.

These 15 Core Operating Principles are the foundational values on which Keyser was built. Keyser's 15 Core Operating Principles encompass my journey, bringing together the lessons my parents taught me about selfless service, my passion for bringing people together, and the understanding that serving others without expectation of return carries with it more riches than we as a culture can understand.

I've also provided additional book recommendations at the end of each section if you would like to dive deeper into any of the topics covered. I only recommend books that I love and have personally found to be extraordinarily helpful to me on my journey. Don't miss out on these great reads!

Jonathan's Book List is #2 in our vault and can be found at: www.ruthlessbook.com/vault.

Let's get started!

PRINCIPLE 1

SELFLESSLY SERVE OTHERS

"We SERVE our clients, partners, and each other fully, self-lessly, and completely and only involve ourselves in projects, activities, and conversations that can truly add value to another individual. We are known by one word—SERVICE— and we live the statement, 'It's not about me.'"

SELF

Selfless service is our first and most important Principle. It is the tenet that permeates all other Principles, but it is also the most necessary at the foundational level. Becoming selfless starts with concerning yourself with the well-being of others without consideration for personal gain.

It is a mindset shift at the very core of your being that motivates you toward self-discovery. Without internalizing a genuine state of selflessness—at a depth that sets aside all expectation of personal gain or return of any kind—this Principle, and all those that follow, will fail.

The journey I shared with you about my life tells you how I came to truly understand and believe in the value of selflessness, both within and acted out in every capacity of life and relationships. How you get there will be different from everyone else because it is your own personal path. You may have similarities in your story to what I experienced, but it may also be that you never found yourself as far down the road of deception and lies that I did. The bottom line is, where do you find yourself now, and if you are being honest, do you live your life to serve others or are you living for yourself? If you recognize that there are elements of both (as most people do), do you want to make a change to become more selfless? In my experience, your individual "want to" has to be strong enough to motivate this shift to selflessness.

TAKING THIS FIRST STEP

Like most things that seem simple, the process of reinventing yourself to become selfless takes time, commitment, and determination and is a lifelong journey. It means prioritizing selflessness within your daily routine.

To take that first step, set an initial goal of selflessly serving one person each day. This may not sound like a lot, but trust me when I tell you that it won't be easy. I'm not talking about going miles out of your way. All it takes is choosing someone you already need to interact with, be it a client, partner, or colleague, and really thinking about what they might need in their life. Feel free to ask questions of them to see what you can uncover. Once you find the right opportunity to help them, offer right then to act on it; or, better yet, simply take action with confidence, knowing you're serving someone fully out of selflessness and kindness. You will be surprised at how powerful that act of service is, both for you and the recipient.

Once you've mastered one act of selfless service each day, begin to up the stakes. Build to two per day, then three per day, and ultimately, a minimum of one selfless act for each and every person you interact with. It is a mindset within every interaction of "How can I selflessly help this person?" versus "What can I get out of this person?"

You may find it difficult to squeeze these goals into your busy schedule. I get it. It was hard for me at first too. What I did was decide to make it my top priority to serve someone first thing every day before I did anything else for myself or my business. That eventually grew to trying to find ways to selflessly serve everyone I interacted with. Today, it requires no thought; it is my natural state of interacting with people, and this is what makes it so powerful. Through routine and discipline, I reprogrammed myself to seek first to serve others in every interaction, and it is exactly that new automatic operating state that has created all my success.

As you begin to set your own goals, look for a rhythm that works best for you. Think about what time of day you can give the most focus to the task you've chosen, and stick to your commitment.

Faith Rocha, who is one of our senior operational stars, has a personal mindset of service with everything she does. She desires deeply to be of service to those around her and as a result, she has become one of the most relied on and trusted people within Keyser. Service in your personal actions creates trust and career opportunities for yourself, and Faith is the perfect example of that.

COMPANY CULTURE

Embedding selfless service into your company's culture is vital to the implementation of all fifteen of the Principles and should start while you're still working on becoming selfless within. Every act in service to others challenges you to make a genuine change internally. Serving those you work closest with on a daily basis allows you to practice selflessness more often and adds a level of trust and value within your team.

In order for selfless service to permeate the entire team, each member must be on their own selfless journey as well, which is why hiring people who are either already selfless or who want to become selfless is so important. It is also key for you and for each person on the team to remember that becoming selfless is a continuous process. Learning to be and remain selfless is a goal to continually strive after.

INTEGRATING SELFLESS SERVICE IN THE OFFICE

One way to work selfless service into your office environment is to start gradually integrating service into your current practices and routines. Whatever you are doing in your regular workday and whatever your meeting schedule looks like, stay with those same processes. The difference is that rather than approaching each interaction with others on your team with a "What can I get out of this?" attitude, approach it with a "What can I do to help, serve, and give to this person?" attitude. This change can make a monumental difference in how you interact with your team and how they interact with each other. A structure of trust and giving will form and grow stronger each day, building a culture on which your team can thrive.

Honestly, as crazy as this sounds, it really is that simple. Externally, you and the team will look the same. Your meeting schedules will be the same, you will be making the same telephone calls, and you will spend the same amount of time writing emails each day. The difference is that your focus will be on how you can give instead of what you can get.

Bring this mindset and spirit of service to every interaction you have. You will quickly learn that a lot more is possible than you ever realized. Once we stop focusing on ourselves, as I had to do, we begin to see unlimited possibilities for service everywhere. All those previously missed opportunities become clearly obvious.

SUPPORT YOUR TEAM TO STRENGTHEN YOUR CULTURE

I remember a friend of mine, Denise, whom I met with and shared this philosophy with. She was fascinated and said she was going to try it. She went back to her company and tried approaching each interaction she had, both within her company and with clients and partners, from a place of selfless service. She later told me it was hard at first because she was so used to thinking about her own needs in interactions, but she pushed those thoughts aside and tried really hard in each conversation to find at least one thing she could do to help the person she was talking to.

She called me a few months later, excited.

"Jonathan!" she exclaimed.

"Yes?" I replied, very interested in what was behind her excitement.

"This selfless service stuff is magic!" she continued. "When I first met with you, I had very few friends within my company, I wasn't hitting my targets, and my last review had been mixed. Since implementing your approach, I feel like everyone at the company loves me. I just crushed my quarterly sales goal, and I was just promoted to a position I never would have thought possible a couple of months ago. I can't believe it was as simple as trying to help everyone I interact with."

It really is that simple. Simple, yet profound, and it requires intentionality, diligence, and commitment.

OPTING FOR A MAJOR SHIFT

Some may decide, as my friend Denise did, to go all in and start selflessly serving everyone she touched. Others may take the "one act of service a day" approach to start. As you read in Part One, being bold and crazy, I personally went all in from the beginning because I wanted the shortest path to success. Remember, and this is no understatement, making a major shift like this is no small or easy task. Take it at whatever pace works best for you, and make sure you do not expect immediate results. They very well may happen like they did for Denise, but with selfless service, you are playing the long game. It is critical to make sure the shift is solid and meaningful and that it's genuine.

CLIENTS AND COLLABORATORS

The fact is, no one wants to "be sold" anything anymore, and no one wants to hear another person pontificate about how great they are and the impressiveness of all their past accomplishments. If you are in a meeting with a colleague and someone goes into that kind of bragging, just redirect the conversation.

"Sales" should not be defined by this exasperatingly inefficient and highly ineffective self-promotion. It is crazy, and it is part of the reason why business is not fun for so many people. Focusing on service is much more enjoyable—and lucrative as well.

People often ask if service means giving to every cause they are asked to contribute to. My short answer is, "Absolutely not!" Service is not defined by giving out money, although it can include that. I am often asked to donate to various causes, and although I love to be generous, I am also careful to clarify for people that "service" doesn't mean I have to give to every cause that asks. In fact, service as I define it within this book has nothing to do with money. True service does not require significant monetary resources. This isn't Christmas, and I'm not Santa Claus.

Keyser service means doing things for others that add value to their lives, either personally or on a business level. It can include money, but there are many other ways to help people as well. I will be giving examples throughout this book of some of those different ways, using stories of actual people serving others.

EXPONENTIAL PAYOFF

The more you serve, the more you gain a reputation for serving. This is how you gain clients. Your advertising becomes, basically, word-of-mouth recommendations from grateful and satisfied partners and clients. This brings more clients, more business, and more money.

Remember, in all your meetings with people, "Not everything is about you." The less you focus on you, the better your relationships will be. Cross over into the other person's world, and focus on what is best for them.

When I first got into commercial real estate, I was told

that cold-calling is an excellent and very productive use of time. I now wholeheartedly disagree, to put it mildly. I see an hour spent strategically helping somebody as far more productive than a hundred hours of cold-calling.

I recently had a conversation on this topic with an influential woman in the marketplace. Melissa said, "Jonathan, it's interesting you would say that [about shifting your focus to others], because I actually did that in a meeting recently. I was trying to get someone to use my services. I looked up on his whiteboard and saw a list of companies he would love to get as clients listed there. So I asked him, 'How can I help you with those? Can I make introductions for you?' We discussed how I could do that for him. The next day, I woke up to seven unsolicited potential client introductions in my inbox from him to *me*."

I said to her, "That's exactly how it works!"

At Keyser, we do that every day, all day, everywhere we go. Can you imagine the number of supporters we gain when people know we are there to serve them?

BE KNOWN FOR SERVING

The same can be true for you. The people you serve become your advocates, and there is no limit to the number of people you can help. They become your evangelists out in the business community, telling others how service oriented you are. This is the best kind of advertising you can ever get. It removes any need to prove yourself or to impress people. You can just show up and serve, and that leads to more opportunities for service and more introductions. People *remember* when they have been selflessly served.

People in our community, from clients to collaborators to other business people, know Keyser as being readily available to help. For example, we frequently receive requests for connections from people looking for work. We don't ask for a finder's fee or anything else in return. We just help people, using our connections to do so. Over the years, we've helped hundreds, if not thousands, of people find work. As a result, many of those we have helped have subsequently referred their companies to us for their commercial real estate needs. We didn't do it to get their business. We did it to help, but often it ends up turning into business for us.

We have had people reach out to us for assistance in getting more connected in the community. Others have contacted us looking to grow their businesses. We find out the kinds of companies they want to serve, and we help make those introductions.

Not long ago, one of the founders of Keyser who lives Principle 1 as good as anyone in the firm, Ian Davie, received an email from one of his contacts containing a list of his top clients for Ian to add to his own contact list. Ian was so surprised that he picked up the phone and called this man to thank him. When he asked what had brought this on, his contact reminded him that Ian had made some very important connections for him about five years earlier, and one of those connections had become his biggest client. Ian had neither asked for nor expected anything in return when he made those introductions. Sending the list to Ian was his contact's way of saying thank you.

With each interaction, listen and focus on how you can help in a way that is meaningful and beneficial, asking for nothing in return.

The opportunities that serving opens up are limitless. You will find that you will not need a sales force. Instead, people will come to *you*, bringing with them more introductions and meetings than you ever expected.

For inspiration to start your selfless service journey, watch Keyser members talk about their experience applying selfless service at work, #3 free item to you in the vault: www.ruthlessbook.com/vault.

Let's get to serving.

KEY PRINCIPLE POINTS

1. Make a commitment to understand, internalize, and integrate authentic selfless service daily into your life.

2. Take the next step to extend and incorporate the selfless service mindset among your team members.

3. Build trust within your company culture so that each person feels supported and will be bold in enforcing Principle 1 with each other and with clients and collaborators.

4. Start by selflessly serving at least one person a day and build to serving in every interaction with someone else.

5. Strategically build a network founded on selfless service.

6. Rather than approaching each interaction with a "What can I get out of this?" attitude, approach it with a "What can I do to help, serve, and give to this person?" attitude.

7. Approach interactions, at all levels, with the mentality of "I want to figure out how I can help you in a way that is meaningful and beneficial to you, and I ask for nothing in return."

BOOKS TO GROW BY

Never Eat Alone by Keith Ferrazzi

This is the book I used as a manual for creating truly meaningful connections leading to referrals. The author, who has now become a friend, provides many practical examples on how to create true, meaningful, long-term relationships.

Give and Take by Adam Grant

This is the best book I have read on the subject of building a business model on selfless service. It separates people into three categories—Givers, Matchers, and Takers—and explains why Givers are both the most and least successful. This is a must-read for anyone wanting to build a selfless-service business model.

OUTWORK THE COMPETITION TO WIN

"We outwork our competition and win as a result. We work relentlessly, tirelessly, and passionately toward our cause and do not allow ourselves to be distracted, discouraged, or deterred from our mission by ANYTHING, no matter how enticing it may appear."

SELF

The basis of this Principle begins within—committing to becoming a person of unrelenting determination, focus, and gratitude. There is a reason why Keyser's tagline is "Relentless Client Champion." In order to be a person relentless in the pursuit of outworking the competition, you must desire results at a deep personal level and have the commitment and resolute drive to make it happen. I will teach you how to create and foster this commitment within yourself within this chapter.

Serving others is not easy. If you've started to do acts of selfless service already, you'll already be facing thoughts such as "Wow, this is great, but when will I see results?" First, as we discussed in Principle 1, stop looking for change in others' actions toward you and focus on the change happening in you. Stick with the process, and remember that it takes time to make selfless service a successful business strategy.

So many people give up, quit, get distracted, or bounce from opportunity to opportunity. Success through service takes time and commitment, which is why this Principle is so important. Don't give up, work tirelessly, and don't worry if it doesn't feel like it is working. This stuff takes time. Focus on doing the right things, and the success will follow in due time.

AN ATTITUDE OF GRATITUDE

You might be wondering why I would start this section out with gratitude. In my opinion, having the staying power to not quit and to outwork the competition day in and day out requires a true attitude of thankfulness. It takes true grit to hang in there day after day without seeing results, so an attitude of gratitude is essential to staying positive and not succumbing to the temptations to quit.

"So how do I do that?" you might wonder. Well, one easy step is to make a daily list of the things you really appreciate. If you cannot think of any, think harder! No matter how bad your situation may be—or how many people question your decision to change to a selfless service business model—there are many things for which to be grateful. The more you focus on those, the more of what you want in your life will show up and the happier you will be.

For the first few years after I changed my personal approach to business to that of focusing on serving, I fought discouragement. There were many times when my body felt like giving up. I was working my hardest, getting totally exhausted, and still not finding success. The nights were especially discouraging as I would often lie in bed staring at the ceiling, wondering if I was crazy.

Every evening, instead of letting stress overwhelm me, I found that it helped to talk to myself. "I am grateful I get to feel good when I go to bed at night. I am grateful for the opportunities I have to serve others. I am grateful for all the amazing things in my life (and then I would list them out loud). I am confident that this business strategy is going to work." Taking that time to be grateful helped keep me going each day.

DEDICATION TO MASTERY

In addition to gratitude, a dedication to mastery is key to true success. Mastery is where the real money resides and where staying the course leads. If you put in only mediocre effort, you should not wonder why you don't achieve extraordinary results. Do not quit before you have had time to become a dominant player in your space. With very few exceptions, all the top players in their fields have spent many years sticking with one thing and working very hard at it, doing the things other people are not willing to do.

Malcolm Gladwell describes this brilliantly in his book *Outliers*. Ten thousand hours of determined effort toward a singular cause, without quitting, is the key to mastery, which if continued leads to extraordinary success in whatever you do. It also keeps you from getting a reputation as someone who is not a serious player. Don't jump from opportunity to opportunity. Stay the course, stick with it, and the more success you have, the more opportunities will naturally come your way.

A friend of mine, Danny, who owns a successful insurance practice, likes to say, "I was never the best insurance guy. I just stuck around long enough to outlast everyone else who quit." There is a lot to be said for this philosophy.

You may be wondering, "How do I motivate myself to

work hard and not quit when the work is tedious and I am not realizing the success I want?"

First, you need to feel a personal alignment with the mission and values of the organization in which you work. If you don't, you may be in the wrong business or wrong company. Misalignment around mission and values drove me to leave my prior company and launch Keyser, and I have never looked back. If you are not aligned within your business, be brave and find or create something that is aligned.

Life is too short to stay somewhere that is not a good fit for you. As Hardison likes to say, "Be the hero, and do the thing you would encourage your kids to do if they were in your situation."

But if you are in a place where you have alignment around mission and values, then the secret is in creating a good plan, being grateful daily, and applying determined and unwavering effort without giving up.

COMPANY CULTURE

This Principle is not about being workaholics—far from it. As any successful and genuine company should, our culture values our families, vacations, personal time, and other worthy pursuits, strongly encouraging our people to take plenty of personal time off. However, we understand the value of effort over and above the norm.

One element that supports Principle 2 is the Pareto Principle, otherwise known as the 80/20 rule. In our industry, for example, this means that 20 percent of brokers earn 80 percent of the fees generated in any given commercial real estate market. This also means that 20 percent of the expended effort in a given market results in 80 percent of the results. So we put in the extra effort and work relentlessly toward our goal because we understand that the fruits of our extra labor will be extremely worthwhile.

We realize that for every ounce of additional effort we exert over our competition, the payback is exponential. And we integrate this Principle throughout our company, each person working as a part of the team to partner with each other and to put our best product before our clients.

DEDICATION TO YOUR TEAM

A very important element of this Principle is remaining focused on our mission and not being tempted by greener grass elsewhere. Don't bounce around from company to company, industry to industry, and career to career, continuously seeking something "better." Don't be tempted by promises and stories from others in different companies or careers. Develop perseverance: pick your horse and stick with it.

Within your team, especially once you've built a level of trust and service to each other, there will also be an expectation that each member will be loyal to the group as a whole. Simply because that level of trust exists, your culture will fly in the face of the bounce mentality that exists in almost every other company in your industry. You're developing long-term relationships and building your team up to be the most successful and selfless resource your clients can benefit from. Simply put, long-term relationships equal long-term success.

The same mentality is necessary regarding your dedication to your staff. Constantly bringing in new staff with the latest-and-greatest degree or certification doesn't guarantee better productivity or success. When you invest in your team, you're investing in the success of your people, your culture, and your company.

"Bouncing around" prevents people from achieving mastery at anything, and companies filled with people who bounce around typically do not become world-class organizations.

CLIENTS AND COLLABORATORS

At Keyser, we serve our clients and external collaborators tirelessly and relentlessly. Sometimes that means getting creative along the way. Ryan Steele, an amazing Keyser team member, was introduced to a prospective client whose company had been trying for several years to find a new location. Because of the intricacies of their needs, none of the three brokerage firms they had already worked with had been able to help them.

When Ryan met with their CFO, he realized right away that using the standard multiple listing services was insufficient for this search. Instead, to find this very unique property, he knew he needed to scour the area the client wanted to be in, parcel by parcel, site by site, studying city and county maps and records, calling local politicians, and reaching out to municipal contacts. In less than a week, he was able to identify an off-market property that met all the client's needs.

As Ryan illustrated in his determination to do whatever it took to solve the client's problem, we at Keyser provide the most comprehensive service levels in the industry. We identify properties for clients that other firms are completely unaware of, and we have done so often enough that we have developed quite a reputation for it.

Because they know this about us, clients who want to

make sure their interests are protected within real estate contracts often ask us to review their leases. Our mission is to make sure our clients' lease agreements protect them as much as possible and significantly limit their liability. This is an area most brokers avoid because it isn't an income-generating task, referring the lease agreement to attorneys instead. The problem is that the attorneys are at a disadvantage because, although they know the intricacies of legal language, they aren't real estate professionals and they weren't involved in negotiating the deal, so there is a gap. Selflessly serving our clients, we spend the extra time to make sure the spirit of the negotiated deal is always in the best interest of the client.

While this is an excellent example of working relentlessly for a client during a transaction, it is important to serve just as tirelessly even when a deal is not involved. Son of Ultimate Coach Steve Hardison and Keyser founding member, Blake Hardison, was once talking with a prospective client when he found out that the man's wife was dying of a rare blood disease. Blake spent the next several days leveraging his relationships trying to track down the top doctor in the state who specialized in that condition.

Eventually, he was able to locate someone who knew the chairman of a health system who ended up facilitating an introduction to the top specialist in the state. Because of Blake's determination, this man and his wife were able to have conversations about her illness with the best doctor possible, one they never would have had otherwise. That, in itself, brought peace for both of them. That's our goal—to be tireless in our efforts to serve. And while it was not Blake's goal to drum up business, that man did eventually become a client; and, of course, he also became a close friend.

The effort you put into serving your clients and prospects will quickly develop your reputation as someone who goes above and beyond the standard job performance in your industry. This reputation is priceless in acquiring future clientele.

DEDICATION WITH RESTRAINT

Let me sidestep for just one moment to offer one *idea you won't hear other people say.* In your desire to put all your effort into your work, there is one thing I do not recommend: do not overprepare for introductory meetings with prospective clients.

I know that sounds crazy. "What do you mean, don't overprepare? I thought I was supposed to be as prepared as possible."

Here is what I have found: if you haven't met the person yet, overpreparing will impede your ability to listen to what the other person is saying. What they say may be very different from the official public story you will find on the internet. I have learned from years of experience that the public impression of a person is often quite different from the real person.

So, yes, prepare for upcoming meetings as best you can, but also bring an open and clear mind to the meeting and focus on the person, listening closely to them. This will open doors to amazing conversations, real understanding, and the best opportunities to meet their true needs.

GRATITUDE TOWARD OTHERS

Remember, this Principle, along with all the others you'll read about, points back to the foundational concept of selflessness. Thinking of others first. In honoring that mindset, remember to show gratitude to anyone who helps you. For example, if someone introduces you to a potential client, make the effort to thank that person. Send a quick note, a text, or an email.

In my experience, a thank-you note is worth its weight in gold. It will not go unnoticed. The person will feel appreciated (in a world where many feel underappreciated), and the cool part is, they will also be much more likely to want to help you again in the future.

Most people are not seeking a referral fee or a gift. They just want to be appreciated.

Make the effort. Write the note. Don't underestimate the power of gratitude. Be relentless and outwork the competition...and *win*!

KEY PRINCIPLE POINTS

1. The relentless pursuit of outworking the competition takes determination and focus.

2. Maintain an attitude of gratitude. Regularly make a list of the things you appreciate in your life. This will help you persevere when you feel like quitting.

3. Work for an organization whose mission and values align with yours.

4. Stay focused on the mission, and don't be tempted by what might look like greener grass.

5. Create a good plan and then apply determined and unwavering effort, going beyond what is expected.

6. Make the effort to express appreciation for what others have done for you. This simplest gesture can be worth its weight in gold.

7. Prepare for introductory meetings with prospective clients, but don't overprepare. Come with a mind to listen and learn in order to respond to their true needs.

BOOKS TO GROW BY

Talent Is Overrated by Geoff Colvin

This book is an eye-opener, revealing that relentless practice is what drives results, not talent or social standing. Your skill and your desire increase over time as you discipline yourself to continue practicing whatever you wish to master.

The Obstacle Is the Way by Ryan Holiday

Many successful people find their greatest successes on the other side of their biggest challenges. Holiday shows us that obstacles are gifts—just a little oddly packaged. Rather than giving up when you are tempted to quit, use the obstacles in your way to drive you relentlessly toward your goal.

TAKE BOLD ACTION, EMBRACING MISTAKES

"We encourage bold action and are not afraid of making a mistake. We never punish mistakes but rather embrace them because to fear mistakes makes a person timid and keeps them out of bold, fearless, massive action, which is precisely where value is created."

SELF

People who spend their time anxiously trying to avoid mistakes end up working well below their true potential. Mistakes—by their very definition—are honest misjudgments, miscalculations, or accidents, *not* ongoing irresponsibility or bad behavior. Allow yourself the freedom to make mistakes without giving the opportunity to harshly criticize and diminish the work you did. Instead, recognize that your attempt failed, but be proud of your effort and willingness to put your best effort out there.

Have a mindset of taking bold action. To me, the fear of messing up or doing something that looks silly or dumb keeps most people from taking bold action and thus achieving true success. Bold action is where successful people live. You want to live there.

Focus on learning from and seeing mistakes for what they really are—opportunities to grow. To reevaluate. To do and be better. And to show you have the grit to make your business thrive. Don't beat yourself up. Only those in action make mistakes; and you want to be in action, not on the sidelines.

COMPANY CULTURE

As a leader or owner, know that punishing mistakes is a recipe for keeping employees in a state of fearful, timid, and unproductive inaction. Punishment, and the fear thereof, only motivates a person to scheme and manipulate the system. The company suffers because it loses its best assets—its confident and productive people. Punishment encourages workers to hide their mistakes when they occur and spend valuable time figuring out how to avoid punishment.

Consider the statements made by Peter Gibbons to Bob Slydell in the classic American comedy *Office Space*:

> The thing is, Bob, it's not that I'm lazy; it's that I just don't care...I have eight different bosses, so that means that when I make a mistake, I have eight different people coming by to tell me about it...My only real motivation is not to be hassled—that and the fear of losing my job. But you know, Bob, that will only make someone work just hard enough not to get fired. I'd say in any given week I probably only do about fifteen minutes of real, actual, work.

Funny, to be sure, but all too true in today's business environment.

Don't expect chastised team members to learn their lessons or perform better in the future. Not at all. What you'll get instead are people who become more cautious, paranoid, insecure, less creative, and only minimally productive.

FAIL FORWARD AND LEARN FROM MISTAKES

Politicians operate under the mantra "When things go wrong, somebody's got to take the fall." At Keyser, though, we have a different philosophy. We recognize that we are all imperfect, we are all trying, and when somebody makes a mistake, we can all learn from it. We commit ourselves to doing our best, and we try to avoid mistakes. We realize that mistakes do happen and they are sometimes costly, but they are part of the deal. We consider mistakes to be gifts that encourage us to grow in our proficiency.

Successful companies learn from their failures. Their acceptance of people making honest mistakes empowers their people to grow. Both the companies and their workers *fail forward* successfully. The question is, what do you want for your team? Consider some of the practices we follow at Keyser.

We've chosen to be very direct with one another, but we are not punishing. What we say is said with love, recognizing the inestimable value of each person and making a commitment to each one's success. That is a very different perspective from the norm.

We also often put younger people in situations that stretch and grow them, and the result is that they learn to take fearless action. When you give people the latitude to make mistakes and *fail forward*, they don't sit in fear. Instead, they challenge themselves and move on.

Punishment is vindictive and is the most ineffective way there is to lead a team. It also creates a culture of fear, name-calling, and backstabbing. Fear of punishment takes all the fun out of the game and causes people to lose productivity. It ultimately undermines the entire culture of your company. Soon, no one is playing to win; everyone is playing *not to lose.*

Don't let your company devolve into one in which the employees are fearful of doing the wrong thing and worried about being berated, driving them to hide out, play it safe, and never demonstrate their true talents. What a shame that would be, both for the individuals and for the company.

PLAY TO WIN

At Keyser, we expect to win, so we play to win. The game element adds energy and fun, eliminating punishment. If someone drops the ball, we send that player right back onto the field with words of encouragement. Our clients win when we all work together, fully supporting one another and learning from our faults rather than punishing them.

When Rick Osselaer, a veteran Keyser member, first started working with us, he accidentally copied a landlord on a confidential email to a tenant client, and the client reached out to me, frustrated. Rick had moved too quickly and had made a mistake. Having come from a more traditional commercial real estate culture, Rick was very worried that when he came into the office, he would get in trouble. But instead, he got a pleasant shock. I looked at Rick and said, "Was that optimal? No. But everyone makes mistakes, and here at Keyser we don't punish mistakes. We learn from them. Correct it and move on!"

Rick was so relieved that he went back to work and immediately corrected the problem. He connected with the client, who was surprisingly gracious, and they continued on with the deal. Rick could not believe there was no office gossip and no repercussions from his mistake. Instead, he was empowered to right the wrong, learn from it, and move forward confidently.

YOU CAN DO IT

At one time, I was too insecure to believe that I was capable of reaching big goals. Maybe you have experienced that same insecurity. But everyone has huge untapped capabilities within them and can have a genuine impact on the world. We help our people and partners believe they are world changers.

When launching Keyser with us, Blake was twenty-five years old and was already procuring and negotiating multimillion-dollar deals on his own. Keyser is not like other firms in which members are required or pressured into bringing senior members into their big deals. Other firms feel that a big deal is too important for a younger guy. We never bought into this. Blake was able to learn and grow at a tremendous rate because he was never forced to rely on anyone else. We were there mentoring and supporting him but let him take leadership roles early on. From day one, we believe that our people are superstars and are up to big tasks. Do not allow fear of mistakes to hold your team back.

Examine your business to determine where you could become bolder. If you run a company, ask your team members whether they feel empowered, regardless of their ages. Analyze their talents to ensure that they are not being underutilized. Remember, when people are working within their area of giftedness, they are motivated to give more to the organization. If you find that a person is gifted in an area outside their official job description, be bold enough to put them in another department. It is amazing how this can reinvigorate workplace stagnation. Everyone wins in an environment where each member of the team loves what they are doing and is motivated to do their best. Mistakes are not punished, and bold actions are encouraged.

CLIENTS AND COLLABORATORS

We want our people to feel safe and trusted. We want them to know they have a significant amount of personal choice in what they do and how they serve their clients. This creates an environment in which people are much happier, more productive, and willing to go above and beyond for their clients and collaborators.

Microchip is a company that has transformed their entire business by adopting this Principle. Recovering from near bankruptcy, they have become one of the most successful companies in their industry, all due to the CEO creating a culture in which mistakes are embraced. Employees are rewarded rather than punished when they admit mistakes quickly. The result is tremendous corporate creativity and unsurpassed success. Michael J. Jones and Steve Sanghi's book *Driving Excellence* tells the story.

Our Keyser team is definitely held accountable to one another in order to minimize recurring mistakes. But we exhibit love without punishment or public embarrassment. For this reason, the team is not afraid to take bold action in creating value for the company and for clients. They feel safe taking calculated risks without fear of reprisal. Team support gives them the freedom and willingness to throw all their effort fearlessly and wholeheartedly into their work, maximizing their productivity and output.

THINK RIDICULOUSLY BIG

It is extremely important to set really *big* goals for ourselves and our organization. When we first launched Keyser, our declaration to everyone who would listen was "We are going to create a *Fortune* 500 company that will reinvent commercial real estate." Many ridiculed us, but we did not let that slow us down. It is clear from history that nothing extraordinary has ever been accomplished by a company without a bold mission—bold enough to invigorate a team of purpose-driven people to come together to accomplish the mission.

You do not want to be a company that sets modest goals under the guise of realism. You will miss out on the enthusiasm and fun of being part of a highly motivated team who accepts challenges and aims high at big, bold targets. Set huge, crazy, and impossible-sounding goals so that when you rise every morning, you are excited to work toward achieving them.

At Keyser, we created a new way of looking at goal setting. First, we created the BHAG (Big, Hairy, and Audacious Goal) of *transforming our whole industry through service.* We took what we thought was a reasonable goal and then took it to the next level. To be bold, you have to push yourself and your team to reach new limits, and then take action.

Then we decided to go further and create an even broader BHAG, called the HHAG (Huge, Hairy, and Audacious Goal). Our aim is now to *transform the entire business world* through selfless service. We are willing to sound crazy by putting a massive goal out there and working together to achieve it because we are confident that we will.

Life is too short to play it safe. Step out and set huge, ridiculous-sounding goals, and then work relentlessly and passionately until they become reality. Trust your creative intuitions, and do not be afraid to sound crazy or unrealistic. Anyone who has changed the world for good had a lot of skeptics, made many mistakes, and experienced many setbacks on their journey. If it was easy, everyone would do it.

Don't take the safe, easy path. Take bold action, and you might even surprise yourself with what you are actually capable of!

KEY PRINCIPLE POINTS

1. A mistake, by its very definition, is an honest misjudgment, miscalculation, or accident, not ongoing irresponsibility, negligence, or intentional bad behavior.

2. Bold, fearless, massive action is the only way to create extraordinary success. Don't let the fear of looking silly, making mistakes, or failing keep you from taking big action.

3. When you do make a mistake, take the opportunity to grow, to reevaluate, and to take the challenge on again and be an overcomer.

4. Empower your people with safety and trust. Allow a significant amount of personal choice in what they do and how they serve their clients.

5. Recognize we are all imperfect. When your team members make mistakes, extend grace and encouragement. Help them learn from their mistakes and avoid repeats in the future. Be determined to fail forward.

6. As a leader, embrace your mistakes—be an example for everyone to see that you know you are not perfect.

7. Hold one another accountable with love, not punishment or public embarrassment.

8. Put a massive goal out there, believe in it, and diligently work to achieve it.

BOOKS TO GROW BY

Shoe Dog by Phil Knight

This is a great read. It shows how Knight achieved success by acting boldly in a number of different ways that would intimidate most people. He acted fearlessly and went for broke and was abundantly rewarded. The book also focuses on mentorship and hiring great people.

Mindset by Carol S. Dweck

This is one of my favorite books of all time. It explains how your mindset is everything and that having a growth mindset versus a fixed mindset enables you to live into a bold future. You can create yourself however you wish. You are limited only by what you believe you can accomplish, and this message is very powerfully articulated. There are very important lessons for parenting in this book as well.

PRINCIPLE 4

EXCEED CLIENT EXPECTATIONS

"We always do our best and produce more than our clients request or expect every single time. We provide the highest quality service, materials, and deliverables to our clients and partners, and nothing is ever done halfway. Everything is done to the very best of our potential."

SELF

This Principle pairs and builds significantly on Principles 1–3. In order to exceed expectations, you have to redefine your own. You have to change how you understand serving others, be relentless in your approach, be willing to make mistakes, reassess the needs of others, and charge the mountain to reach new heights.

As stated before, this is not an easy path. There is no shortcut or free pass. It is a choice you must make to outperform the competition. It takes commitment and determination. Change starts within, and you have to be willing to go all in. Set extraordinarily high standards for your service levels to your clients, work crazy hard, and commit to doing everything you do to the very best of your abilities. If you do that relentlessly without giving up, you will grow and excel much quicker than those around you. Ultimately, if you do this, there will be no stopping you in the success you can attain, both personally and professionally.

You will wake up one morning and you will be the best.

COMPANY CULTURE

When I'm considering who I want to bring onto my team, I focus on those who are best-in-class and have the right mindset. I care far less about what school they went to and what their historical track record looks like but rather look for a great attitude that I can nurture and develop. When your team is filled with people who have a great mindset, it leads to continual improvement and constant accountability. Our goal is not only to be the best-in-class but also to be constantly pushing the limits, ensuring that we are working to our highest potential, both as individuals and as a firm.

QUALITY PEOPLE

The level of quality starts with the kind of people we hire. To make certain that we can always build quality relationships with our clients and go beyond their expectations, we always prioritize finding culturally aligned members of the team. We hire members who epitomize the Keyser Principles, first and foremost. Experience is important, but alignment is everything. The greatest asset we deliver to the marketplace is our people, not the collateral materials or services.

We maintain a team of individuals who are committed to our mission of changing the world through selfless service. We are all willing to work hard toward that goal and are motivated to put in the extra work necessary to deliver excellence.

Darius Green, one of my best friends and fellow founding Keyser member, gave us an example of providing more value to those we encounter, regardless of whether they are a client or partner. One of his contacts asked for Darius's quick professional opinion on a matter. He could have responded with a simple email, briefly summarizing his professional opinion. However, even though he had no potential prospect of gaining them as a client, Darius sent a full report at no cost with examples supporting his data.

Similarly, a large tech company gave three leases for

review to Matthew Cummings, one of Keyser's smartest and hardest working brokers (and also Keyser's best ping-pong player). Matthew abstracted all three leases, created an executive summary, and then met with their VP of Finance. His presentation revealed opportunities to improve their current lease agreements. He also shared how we could implement a system that would make their commercial real estate portfolio more uniform, systematic, and process oriented.

Matthew's proposal included a suggestion for a full-service advisor rather than a mere transaction manager. This new position would provide a service well beyond that of a typical commercial real estate broker. Matthew's creative, unconventional suggestion, combined with his commitment to producing more than his client requested, gained him a national client.

Because of this best-in-class approach, our team delivers the best products and services possible. Taking the time to be thoughtful and intentional about what we deliver to our clients lets them know they can always expect the best from us. This is incredibly important if we are to maintain our reputation in the market as a best-in-class service organization.

Shoddy deliverables that are poorly or hastily constructed are unacceptable to a firm committed to providing best-in-class service to each and every client. If we anticipate that we will not be able to complete an assignment to its maximum potential, we will not take it on.

The entire Keyser team is committed to helping one another deliver the highest quality products and services possible. Mike Hirth, another of Keyser's amazing brokers, for example, had a client who called him requesting to tour potential building options that same afternoon. Rather than hurriedly pulling and binding property information, two team members took the extra time and effort to compile it properly and put a professional tour book together in real time, ensuring that we could present the clients with Keyser-quality materials for the tour. This kind of team support from other brokers in the office is unheard of in traditional brokerage environments and is one of the things that makes Keyser so special.

CLIENTS AND COLLABORATORS

Quality control is one of our highest priorities, and it ties into our overarching goal of providing best-in-class service to each and every client. Unfortunately, the commercial real estate industry is known for doing the minimum amount required to get paid. This is so commonplace that few clients expect much else from typical commercial real estate brokers.

At Keyser, we see this as a great opportunity to go above and beyond in our service to our clients and collaborators. We seek ways to anticipate their needs before they express them. This level of service requires intentionality, creative thought, and a commitment that persists even when shortcuts look tempting.

We are committed to excellence and are always on the lookout for better ways to deliver value to our clients. As the business world continually changes around us, we want to adapt our methods and improve our abilities. Everywhere we go, we ask ourselves these questions: How can we do better? How can we ensure that we are always leading the market and providing additional value to our clients and partners? Rather than use this commitment to constantly compete within our own company and against our own team members, the Keyser Way is to use our excellence to build one another up and create a better level of service for all of our clients.

There's also another advantage to providing ridiculously high levels of service. Our competitors in the marketplace know that we provide such a high level of service to all of our clients. As such, it is demotivating for them to try to win business over us because they know they will have to produce an unreasonably high level of service just to match what we are providing.

QUALITY RELATIONSHIPS

Mikey Maynard, founder of Keyser Business Advisory Services and human capital guru, adds a different perspective to this Principle that warrants mention here. He emphasizes that the most important element in business is the quality of your relationships with your clients, collaborators, and the people within the community. This means a desire to understand our clients' worlds and a commitment to always deliver top-quality products and services to them.

Part of the mantra of our firm is to take an extraordinary amount of time on the front end of an assignment with new clients in order to understand all aspects of their organizations. We work hard to figure out what they actually *need*. Keyser is not here for simply taking orders. We ask the tough questions and dive deep into their worlds, and then we serve their real needs. As always, we do more than our clients expect.

Once you decide that you want to be the best in your industry, take a good look at your competition. Figure out who is producing the best quality services and deliverables. Set their quality as a *minimum* standard for yourself and your company. Analyze what customers expect from someone in your profession and brainstorm ways to exceed these expectations.

Then do it and don't quit. It's that simple.

KEY PRINCIPLE POINTS

1. There is no shortcut or free pass. Change starts within, and you have to be relentlessly committed to making that change.

2. Highest quality comes from a team dedicated to collaboration.

3. Create a team culture that encourages each person to step out, and help one another to achieve that higher level of service.

4. Hire individuals who are committed to your mission and are willing to work hard towards your goals.

5. Commit to delivering a product and service that is truly your best.

6. If you anticipate that you will not be able to complete an assignment to its maximum potential, do not take that job at all.

7. Always do your very best. Be constantly seeking ways to anticipate your clients' needs and be on the lookout for ways to deliver better value to your clients.

8. Serve people even if they are not your clients. In serving others, you are building relationships of trust, service, and community.

BOOKS TO GROW BY

The Speed of Trust by Stephen Covey

Covey describes how integrity, intent, capabilities, and results are all essential to establishing credibility. Together, they boil down to character and competence. Our prospective clients need to trust us right away if we ever expect them to open up to us and allow us to best serve them. Those who can establish trust quickly *win*. That's why I highly recommend this book.

Getting Naked by Patrick Lencioni

This is a short, easy-to-read business fable that I love. *Getting Naked* is not only a great title for a business book, but it is a great visual for how vulnerability and going above and beyond for potential clients—even before being hired—is critical to success. The way to delight potential clients is to be humble, selfless, and transparent. Only then will they truly open up and enable us to serve them beyond what anyone else will.

PRINCIPLE 5

EXPECT TO WIN BY BEING THE BEST

"We expect to win every single time. Period. We do this because we think and act as we truly are—the best in the business. No one delivers better service or representation than our team. We are the BEST, and we honor ourselves, our partners, and our clients by being and doing our best."

SELF

When we talk about being the best, we're not talking about being boastful or pompous. We're talking about knowing what level of service we need and aim to provide, and then getting it done by being the best at what we do. That drive must begin at an internal level for each person. Without the desire to win by honoring ourselves and others, we lack the motivation that is rooted in self-less service.

Commitment to the success of those we do business with drives us to provide extraordinary results for each and every client. To be truly great at what we do is our highest form of service. For us, "good enough" is not good enough. Being the best is a commitment we make to ourselves and to one another.

For me, I decided at a young age that I was going to be the best. I didn't even know what that meant at the time, but I was committed to it, and I got up every morning and worked extremely hard toward that goal. When discouragement, mistakes, failures, and disappointments happened, I didn't give up. I stayed committed to my decision to be the best.

The coolest part is that being the best really isn't a comparison to others, even though it sounds that way. It really is comparing you against your own potential. Being the best is a mindset. I know many talented brokers who sell themselves short because they don't believe they can be the best and play at the highest levels. Don't sell yourself short. Determine to be the best and then do what is necessary to achieve that.

COMPANY CULTURE

Within a company culture, the attitude of being the best is contagious. We at Keyser know that we are the best. As a result, we hire and keep only top talent, and everyone is challenged to play at the highest levels. That attitude of being the best is part of why so many brokers apply to join our firm. They know we are the best, and so they want in. We say no to many people who want to join us because we want only the very best individuals who are aligned with our core values and willing to work hard and live our 15 Core Operating Principles.

I am personally very grateful there are so many other traditional commercial firms out there that are willing to hire people who either wouldn't be a fit at Keyser or who simply can't cut it at Keyser. Most of our competitors just want to fill seats. We don't. We want only extraordinary, talented people who actually care about others, so we are extremely selective with members of our team. We are the best, and we want only members of the team who believe that and live into that each and every day.

BEING THE BEST BY HELPING CLIENTS BE THE BEST

To our knowledge, Keyser is the only commercial real estate tenant firm that also has a human capital practice, assisting clients with the development of their leaders and employees. Mikey and his Business Advisory Services team at Keyser specialize in this aspect of our company. We assist clients in developing people within their organizations, and we facilitate the training of leaders and employees to maximize their potential.

For most organizations, real estate and facilities is their second or third largest expense, with the largest line item being their people. We made the decision to add a human capital practice within Keyser so that if we cannot help someone with their real estate challenges, we can still help them with the people side of their business. The great advantage to clients in upgrading their human capital—creating a culture of quality—is that they will see their revenues go up; they may see their operating expenses go down as well if they also hire us on the real estate front. We want to help our clients be the best at what they do by our team being the best at what we do.

> Improve your bottom line by using Keyser's three-step talent action plan, #4 in the vault: www.ruthlessbook. com/vault.

CLIENTS AND COLLABORATORS

Expecting to win is just a different way of looking at service. It is being committed to go above and beyond the industry expectations. Simply by paying attention and looking intently for opportunities to serve, we develop an advantage on a personal level that most businesses don't have. We also look out for prospective clients' interests as well as those of the people and businesses we connect with because we are committed to their success. We care about the people we come in contact with and are committed to serving them to the very best of our abilities.

BE-THE-BEST MENTALITY IMPRESSES THE BEST CLIENTS

Andrew Laporte, a Keyser rising star, explains it well: "Being the best in all we do is a Keyser mentality. Whether trying to gain or to serve a client, we are determined to exceed their expectations. We will customize the service to each and every client, and we will never deviate from our commitment to providing the best possible service." Consider how you can establish the best practices in your industry, then adapt to each client's needs, always keeping to your high standards.

As weird as this sounds, many salespeople feel that they aren't good enough for certain big accounts. Nonsense! Don't waste your valuable time feeling insecure that maybe another firm or person is better suited than you to help a potential client. If you are willing to outwork and outdeliver your competitors, then you do deserve their business. Fear of rejection will take you out of the game and never create greatness. People sense confidence, and nothing creates more confidence than extraordinary commitment to a client's success.

We expect to win every single time. We want people to see and experience the sincerity and authenticity of our team, a team totally committed to our clients' success. We value every person, company, and relationship. With this mindset, why would we ever lose?

When we are 100 percent committed to the success of our clients and we have extensive expertise and experience, we provide best-in-class service and we walk into the room truly believing we will win.

When we meet with a client, we are not timid. Keyser Franchise Services Team Leader Ty Brewster had a meeting set up with a significant potential client. When he walked into the meeting, he simply *assumed* this was going to be his client. Ty started helping him immediately by identifying three things he needed and then got to work. He didn't ask for or wait for the go-ahead; he just proceeded as if he were already their guy. The result? He got the client's business.

We want our clients to know we work hard for them. Our goal is to deliver better materials, use better negotiating strategies, and ultimately, secure the best terms possible in each transaction. We take time to really get to know our clients so we can effectively provide the deals that best meet their individual needs.

WE WIN WHEN THEY WIN

Keyser is strategically (long-term) driven rather than tactically (short-term) driven in our business practices. While other firms typically look at real estate transactions tactically, Keyser looks more broadly to analyze how to maximize our clients buying power while strategically lower their operating expenses. This Principle is not about people expecting to win a deal but rather winning by ensuring long-term success for our clients.

We owe our clients the opportunity to work with the best possible commercial real estate and business consulting firm, one that works hard to deliver results that exceed their expectations. That is who we are—every single time.

We expect to win by diversifying what we do. We expect to win by ensuring that the client wins.

The other side of this winning equation is knowing when to say no. We don't waste our time pursuing business that we do not think we are going to win or for which we do not feel we are the best fit. We do not typically do requests for proposals, as those are not relationships but rather vendor-style arrangements where it is all about lowest cost. We spend our time on clients and people who are aligned with our mission and whom we choose, knowing we can serve them best.

We are told that our brokers are more confident than most. When we walk into a meeting, we go with the mindset that we are going to *win*. It's not cocky. It's committed. And we are committed to serving relentlessly to get there.

KEY PRINCIPLE POINTS

1. Being the best is a mindset that is intentionally created and perpetuated.

2. Be the company that is so committed to service that you outperform all other companies in your field.

3. Expect to win by being the most committed to your potential clients.

4. Assume you already have a prospect's business, and show up committed to serving them to the best of your ability.

5. Evaluate whether there are additional services you can add to meet the needs of your clients.

6. Be strategic, not tactical.

7. Recognize when you are not the best fit for a client or they are not the best fit for you, and don't waste time with the wrong relationships.

BOOKS TO GROW BY

Relentless by Tim S. Grover

This book describes my approach better than any other book I have ever read. Grover writes about his work with Michael Jordan, Kobe Bryant, Dwyane Wade, and Charles Barkley, especially noting their obsessive pursuits of excellence. Never satisfied, the relentless person expects to win by striving endlessly to be the best. They do whatever it takes with relentless effort and continual growth to position themselves to win. Awesome book.

Grit: The Power of Passion and Perseverance by Angela Duckworth

Grit is a great book that encapsulates two of our Keyser Principles, Principles 2 and 5. Passion and perseverance enable people to become the best. You do what you enjoy and keep going, even when it is difficult. Greatness is achieved through effort and commitment to being and becoming the best. Those who achieve mastery win more often than those who do not. I want to win. Every time. Love this book.

PRINCIPLE 6

TRULY ONE TEAM

"We are one team, and each person plays an integral role. Together, we are more successful than we would be on our own, and we honor the importance of everyone's contribution. We each serve a critical team function, and no team member is superior to another."

SELF

We have a significant competitive advantage at Keyser. Once you have the opportunity to join Keyser, every other member of the team is committed to making you extraordinarily successful at the individual, team, and company level. This may sound like a cliché, but it is true, and it is a critical part of the culture we have created. As I've said and will continue to say throughout these Principles, each person makes all the difference for the company, and that difference begins within the person.

INDIVIDUALS BUILD A TEAM

We are growing the model of a service-based business with our talented and driven team members, working to bring these Principles to life. It is much better to work with a community of like-minded individuals than to forge a path alone.

Think back to my experiences working with traditional brokerage firms, before starting Keyser. I was constantly fighting over deals, protecting my client information, and looking over my shoulder. This is the world most brokers operate in. But the longer I've been in business and the more my team implements these Principles, the greater the evidence shows that the dog-eat-dog mindset is counterproductive to true, long-term, sustainable success in business.

COMPANY CULTURE

Within Keyser, each person's contribution is equally and critically important, unlike other businesses that are known for their well-defined hierarchy. Elsewhere, the contributions of "junior" or "less-tenured" brokers are regularly discounted until they have "earned" the right to be treated as peers by senior brokers or consultants—and even then, the cutthroat mindset continues. This demoralizing situation leads to dysfunctional behavior and creates a strong sense of "us versus them." It ensures that people will continue to ruthlessly compete and undermine each other in a zero-sum game, similar to a real-time, adult version of the children's game King of the Hill. That's not a productive growth mindset for any individual or company. And that's exactly what we want to change.

BORROWED WINGS

There are many benefits to treating everyone as an equal in a supportive and collaborative structure; however, the greatest benefit is that it empowers the next generation of up-and-coming superstars to achieve their own greatness much sooner. Rather than feeling demeaned and "less than" for the first ten or fifteen years of their careers, they are treated as integral parts of the team from the beginning.

As a new broker with Keyser, industrial specialist Kari Hartman found it very helpful in her first few weeks with us to be encouraged to sit down with key members of the team and learn some of their best practices. The Keyser team philosophy enables veteran brokers to let down their guard without fear that new hires are going to become their competitors. Consequently, expertise and advice flow openly in our collaborative environment. All new Keyser members like Kari know they can lean on anyone in the office for guidance and support. This is an invaluable gift, especially for someone new to the industry.

At Keyser, our senior people take the junior members under their wings. New members are encouraged to sit down with *all* the senior members and learn how to be successful. Our goal is to train our young people to use the best strategies known and be as effective as possible.

This egalitarian, supportive behavior is unique to our industry. Nationwide, over 80 percent of newcomers who try to become real estate brokers give up and drop out because this is such a difficult business and they get so little support as they try to climb the ladder.

CLIENTS AND COLLABORATORS

When Keyser franchise specialist Joe Pillor was new to Keyser, he used this collaborative philosophy as a selling point. Joe shared with contacts that "one of the values we bring to the table is that you're not just working with me. There are centuries of experience among our brokers, who bounce ideas off one another and help one another move a deal forward."

Clients who hire Keyser acquire more than one broker;

they acquire the expertise of the whole firm helping them both directly or indirectly. This can happen only in a collaborative team environment like ours.

This upbeat, synergistic team atmosphere is what drew Patti Gentry, an industry veteran, to Keyser. Being one team energizes her and creates a desire to come to the office every day. Knowing that she can ask anyone for help or information is something she could never do at any of her previous nationally recognized firms. In Patti's own words, "Here, it is not about egos, commissions, or titles. It is all for the benefit of the client."

CHANGING BUSINESS FOR CLIENT SUCCESS

You will notice on our website that we are not a big fan of personal titles. We each have our role, but we don't rely on egocentric titles. This supports the "one team" concept and reminds us that we are equal—everyone's contribution is important. From our receptionist, who gives the first impression of our firm, to everyone who enters or calls, to the brokers or consultants who have been here the longest, we are all equal. We all work together, coaching one another and treating one another as equals.

When skilled broker Nathan Pancrazi joined Keyser as a new team member, we included him on a sizable prospective client project. We gave Nathan a speaking portion in the presentation and gave him a significant role in pulling the project together. When we won the client, we were intentional about giving Nathan a lot of credit, and we celebrated him. That intentional process in our office gives new team members increased motivation to excel.

We view our firm as an elite group who works collaboratively as an organization, expects a lot from each member, and is exceptionally capable—similar to the attitude of Navy SEALs. If you met a SEAL, you would not ask, "What rank are you?" You would just say, "Wow, you are a SEAL!" The membership is all you need.

We are a specialized, highly talented flat organization without rank, titles, or a tiered management chart. My role as servant leader is to serve each and every member of the team and help everyone to attain absolute success. That is the goal of every other team member as well.

This "flat structure" has been used by other highly successful companies as well. For example, Google utilizes the flat structure by encouraging employees to make decisions without having to seek permission from "upper" levels of management. This technique allows the employees at Google to feel they are personally responsible for the decisions they make, which empowers them to make decisions carefully. They feel that the management team trusts them, and therefore they live up to that confidence by performing at their best.

We encourage similar practices at Keyser, with the goal of making our members feel they are being treated as fully capable parts of the team at all times.

To be very clear, Keyser is not a company that operates with a socialist mentality, giving everyone handouts regardless of value provided. Everyone receives fair compensation for the value they bring.

Operating as one unified team with everyone contributing generously to one another's success is how we create an equal playing field for ourselves. All of us end up making more money than we would have made on our own, and together, we draw closer to our goal of changing the business world through selfless service.

KEY PRINCIPLE POINTS

1. Treat everyone as an equal, no matter the role, tenure, or status of their position.

2. Encourage your team to commit to helping every other team member become extraordinarily successful. The desire to be competitive will be as a team taking on the industry, not as one team member against another.

3. Create a synergistic team atmosphere that draws veteran talent that is philosophically aligned, allowing them to feel confident that their knowledge and experience can help the company and team grow and become a stronger entity in the industry and for clients.

4. Consider creating an organizational structure in your company that will empower employees to take charge, help make decisions, and feel responsible for the company's success.

5. Create a collaborative team environment so clients feel they are hiring your whole team, not just an individual.

BOOKS TO GROW BY

Leaders Eat Last by Simon Sinek

This is an extraordinary book about selfless leadership and the self-interest embedded within it. The title says it all—real leaders put their people first, care more about their success than their own, and make them feel safe. Real leaders look at themselves as servants of their people. They treat people like family and look after their long-term interests, and they make them want to never leave. This book is worth reading more than once.

Conscious Capitalism by John Mackey and Raj Sisodia

In addition to launching the Conscious Capitalism movement, Mackey and Sisodia—through this book—pioneered a philosophy of business as a driver for good in the world. There are many excellent takeaways, but my favorite is relative to Principle 6 in that it encourages treating your people like shareholders, helping them find meaning within the organization, empowering them to succeed and flourish in a supportive way, treating everyone as valuable, and not having a leadership mindset of superiority. Mackey has also become a personal friend, and I can vouch that he lives what he preaches.

GIVE FIRST

"We give first, fully and exuberantly, knowing that if we focus on giving and truly seeking opportunities to help others in real, tangible ways, then we experience true joy and fulfillment in our own lives, and as a side benefit, we experience resounding success as well."

SELF

Principle 1 focused on selfless service. This Principle is about giving gifts to others that will amaze them, wow them, and bless them.

It's easy to find ways to give to others, and the more generously and creatively you give, the bigger the impact you will have. Don't misunderstand. I am not saying to go give all your money away. That is not what I am talking about here. Sometimes I give money when I believe that will have the biggest impact, but I like to give very creative and thoughtful gifts that massively impress people and that have a huge impact.

One of our future stars, Chase Wilson, has this down pat. He figures out whom he wants to do business with, researches them until he finds something that would be a hugely meaningful gift, and then creates and gives it to them. He looks for something that will have emotional impact—something from their past or one of their passions that he can custom design an amazing gift around.

These gifts are not usually expensive. Just very customized and thoughtful. The best part—he does it anonymously and then a few weeks later follows up. It is amazing the impact these thoughtful gifts have, and almost always, he gets the meeting and usually the business as well.

We have other fantastic examples you can work from, #5 in the vault. Go to www.ruthlessbook.com/vault for some creative gifting ideas you can use to help you get started giving gifts today.

Get good at identifying ways that giving something tangible to someone will have a big impact. Nothing is cooler than getting a gift, especially one that is customized and unexpected. Powerful gifting is one of the great secrets to unlocking great relationships. Become good at giving, and you will find that others will give what you want to you more generously than you ever thought possible.

Giving doesn't always have to be an actual gift either. Giving someone the credit can make a friend for life. Giving of your time, your energy, your relationships, your empathy all have an impact. The key is keeping yourself constantly looking for ways to give to others.

As you can imagine, if everyone waited for someone else to be the first to act, we would all be at a standstill. So in order to put selfless giving in motion, you have to make the first move. By developing that new habit, over time, you'll be able to give without keeping track or even caring whether or not people reciprocated.

RECIPROCATE BY PAYING IT FORWARD

Having a philosophy of "paying it forward" helps with maintaining the right mindset as you give to others selflessly. Rather than expecting others we have helped to repay us, we want those we freely help to do the same for someone else. Paying it *forward*, as we hope people will do, becomes similar to a small stream turning into many rivers as it branches ever outward. People freely help others, who in turn freely help others, who in turn freely help others. Paying it forward enables many people to receive the help they need and then energizes them to experience the joy of giving as well. As an added bonus, you know that you had a hand in helping create that positive and constant flow of generosity among the people you know and, by extension, touched the lives of strangers down the line.

Here is the thing: it is so hard when you have bills to pay to give to others without expectation of a return. Don't misunderstand me. You *can* expect a return—that is the whole point of this book; just expect a return of long-term, sustainable success, not an immediate quid pro quo reciprocation of each gift you give, or you will get frustrated and give up long before it comes back to you. That is the difference. Giving selflessly leads to returns that often come from unlikely sources, so give selflessly and be grateful when a gift comes back to you from someone you never expected. Life cannot handle an imbalance, and giving to others pays it forward into the universe. If you do it enough, eventually it comes back to you, the giver, in spades.

BENEFITS THAT CREATE RELATIONSHIPS

In many instances, acting in selflessness can create opportunities that go beyond a simple moment of kindness. Once I decided to switch to a service-first model, I began to experience benefits that helped create opportunities for others and for myself in turn. Far greater than I ever would have thought possible.

Blake Hardison, one of our own Keyser members, is an example of this. In the years before we started our own company together, Blake was actually a competitor of mine. I began coaching him on service ideas and introducing him to prospective clients, collaborators, and people of influence in the community, without regard for the possibility that he could take clients away from me. I gave clients and relationships to him freely first and did so happily, not expecting anything in return.

Blake was so impressed with my acts of selfless giving that he decided to join me, and today he is one of our top producers and a leader within our company.

COMPANY CULTURE

Naturally, when you interact with others who are aligned with the give-first mindset, each person constantly looks for ways to help one another, and that creates powerful and effective organizations. Bonds of trust form. Clients sense it. Recruits sense it. And before you know it, more clients want to hire you and more top talent wants to join your organization. This is why it's so imperative that each person on your team makes the daily effort to interact with one another with a give-first attitude.

THE PLEASING PRISON

Many people do something that looks very similar to living the give-first mindset, but what they are actually doing is something called the *pleasing prison*. It is the place in our minds where we subject ourselves to doing only what will gain us the approval of others. When I wanted business before my transformation, I was stuck in this prison. I would take steps to make it look like I was giving to others, but what I really was doing was trying to gain approval, business, or favor from others by appearing to give selflessly.

The pleasing prison is creepy and uncomfortable for all parties involved. It is easy to sense, and it steals all the power from the giving. When we're trapped in this prison, we live our lives trying to impress a specific group of people. We are inauthentic and motivated by the expectations we put on others, which is a miserable and ineffective way to live. People pleasers feel an inescapable desperation to gain approval, even to the point of compromising their values, integrity, and, potentially, even their closest relationships.

My escape from this prison took place when I began to give fully to others without desiring anything in return. I began to experience *freedom*—along with deep satisfaction, success, and meaningful relationships.

The concepts of serving and pleasing may look deceptively similar, but they are miles apart in origin and in productivity. "People pleasing" typically comes from insecurity, fear, or personal, selfish ambition, and it is all about outward appearances. True service comes from a caring heart.

The two also produce different results in both the giver and the receiver, ending in either tension or gratitude. The two concepts feel different, not only to the giver but also to the receiver, even if only on a subconscious level. When people sense you are trying to manipulate them for your own benefit, there is tension. On the other hand, when people realize that you truly care about them, with no thought for yourself, they feel a deep appreciation. This is where having a solid foundation of give-first service becomes so important as you serve your team and, further, serve others in your life and business.

CLIENTS AND COLLABORATORS

One of our missions at Keyser is to help our team learn the difference between selfless giving and pleasing. We constantly remind members of our team to be aware of which choice they are making in any given situation—giving and serving, or just pleasing others. This distinction is critical in deciding whether to give of your time and money to a nonprofit organization, helping someone with a few introductions, or giving someone a meaningful gift. We say, "Ask yourself, 'Is this activity bringing me joy?' If not, then you are probably acting from a place of insecurity, manipulation, or with an ulterior motive."

Understanding the difference can be challenging. I have had people try out our system and then come back in disappointment because it did not bring them immediate financial gain. They will say, "I guess we just need to be patient." Whenever I hear that phrase, I know that the person does not understand what we do. What are they being patient for? The reward? The payoff? If they have truly served or given to someone—genuinely and selflessly—*the reward is contained in the act.*

A CONTRAST TO THE GIVE-FIRST MINDSET

After I had explained our selfless giving business strategy to a group of entrepreneurs, the owner of the business where we were gathered spoke up enthusiastically.

"Jonathan I really appreciate you sharing what you are up to. I want you to know that we have exactly the same business model as you do."

"Really?" I replied. "Please tell me more."

"Well, helping others is a key component to our business model too. See, look at these words on the wall."

At this point she showed me a manifesto containing their core values. She continued,

"We always try to go out of our way to give to everyone who helps us, and we teach our people to really help our clients."

"No offense," I replied, "but you have actually the opposite business model from ours. You think that helping others who help you is unique and that taking care of your clients is going above and beyond. Again, no offense, but that is what everyone does. I actually am describing something very different.

"You see, I am describing a model in which you do not worry about your own needs at all. You do not monitor what you do for other people in order to compare it to what they have done for you or even concern yourself with what they could do for you in the future."

Now that I had their attention, I continued, "What you are describing, though it may not be intentional, is selfish and manipulative behavior repackaged to look like selfless giving. What I am talking about is pure giving of yourself to others. This means pouring your energies and resources and relationships into helping all the people you touch in as many ways as you can, and then getting up the next day and doing it all over again. That is what I am describing, and that is precisely the mindset that leads those who follow it to extraordinary success and wealth."

"Well, how do you make any money, then?" she asked. "If you spend all your time giving to and helping other people, won't you end up like Mother Teresa? Happy but broke?"

"Great question," I replied. And then I told them how we do business and how it creates committed relationships that lead to truly sustainable business success. Once I was able to help them see the flaw in their approach, I was then able to help them see the true nature of the give-first mindset. It changed the way they looked at everything.

GIVE-FIRST MINDSET WITHIN THE KEYSER TEAM

Making the give-first mindset an integral part of your company's core principles can easily sound counterintuitive, but let's dig a little deeper into the heart of the matter. Let me give you a couple of examples to consider.

One of our competitors recently negotiated a lease for a certain company, and the lease was declared by the broker to be ready for execution. It was a horrible deal that would have put the business in a risky financial position. However, the broker was unwilling to renegotiate because a better deal would mean that he would receive a lower commission. Thankfully, members of that company were introduced to Chelsea Austin, who is the head of Keyser's healthcare practice group. Because of Chelsea's reputation of selfless service, Chelsea's client was confident in referring them to her. She helped renegotiate the lease and improved it immensely for the client—and did it without expectation of a commission. She did it just to help and be of service.

The crazy part is that this company was growing quickly and would have many future opportunities for potential commissions. Because the other broker was unwilling to put the client's best interest over his own and Chelsea was, her give-first mentality gained Chelsea that company as her client for their next leases. This was her reward for her innate desire to help others and her refusal to sit idly by as another company provided subpar service.

Another example of the give-first methodology involved helping a family member of a client. Clint Hardison, a Keyser founding member, was willing to help a client whose son needed a job. Clint spent considerable time figuring out what the young man wanted to do for a career, and then he personally put him in touch with contacts at various companies that were hiring for his desired position. When the young man received a job offer and accepted, the client was overwhelmed with gratitude for Clint's selfless act of service. He graciously wrote Clint a heartfelt letter to thank him for what he had done. Making the initial introductions did not mean that the client's son would get the position, but the act spoke volumes to the boy's father. Selfless serving takes a willingness to give first to another person.

We do this type of giving all the time. Jim Sadler, one of Keyser's senior leaders, gives of his time constantly. He is one of the busiest guys in the company, and he spends a significant amount of time finding ways to selflessly give not only of his time but also of his expertise and resources. It is exactly this mindset that makes him successful and one of Keyser's top leaders. He is always quick to raise his hand to help or give of himself.

As brokers, our time is the most valuable asset we have, and yet Keyser people selflessly give of their time, energies, creativity, and resources to help others.

A culture and company foundation of selfless giving results in a reputation of trust, integrity, and approachability that people are hungry for. Letting go of the need to gain financially from any and every interaction allows you to find joy in serving others from a deeper and humbling place within. And that joy will radiate out into the community and grow like a wildfire.

KEY PRINCIPLE POINTS

1. Do not wait for others to help you; rather, find a way to give to them first without a personal agenda.

2. Paying it forward helps everyone experience the joy of giving by integrating selfless giving into their own businesses. Rather than waiting for or expecting an act of repayment, you are freeing yourself and others to give and serve others.

3. If you think you are in a pleasing prison, ask yourself, "Is this activity bringing me joy?" If not, move from pleasing to serving.

4. The reward of selflessly serving is found in the act of giving first. If you are taking steps to implement this methodology and find yourself impatient with the process, step back and evaluate where your motivations lie.

5. The service first model is more than a novel way of doing business. It is a business model that puts the value of people and their needs above the bottom line.

BOOKS TO GROW BY

Giftology by John Ruhlin

I met Ruhlin through Conscious Capitalism, and he has become a wonderful friend. His book is awesome. In very simple and practical ways, he describes how to leverage selfless giving as a tool for creating value in business. Packed with tips, this is a must-read for anyone looking for ways to delight prospects, customers, or employees with thoughtful and unexpected gifts.

The Go-Giver by Bob Burg and John David Mann

Another short read in parable form, this book outlines the five laws for Stratospheric Success. Basically, Burg and Mann say, the more you give in value than you receive, the more successful in the long term you will be. Bottom line: the more you put others' interests first, the more success you will have.

PRINCIPLE 8

BE YOUR WORD

*"We always follow through with the commitments we make...
ALWAYS. People can rely on us because we do what we say
we will do, and when we see that we cannot, we quickly clean
it up. We are our word, and as a result, what we speak into
existence actually occurs for us."*

SELF

It is not often that you find people who are known for
keeping their word, consistently doing what they say they
will do, even if it is inconvenient or causes them to miss
a bigger opportunity. Today's general standard seems to
be the opposite, with most people considering it unnecessary to always do what they say, especially if they have
a "good enough" excuse not to. This lower standard is
so prevalent today that we have come to accept it, both

from ourselves and from others. We've deteriorated the meaning of integrity, in turn sabotaging our own success.

People have said to me about this point, "But, Jonathan, everyone does this! This is just our culture. No one does what they say they will do anymore." Exactly!

The truth is that the *internal* impact of not keeping our word is even more damaging than the external implications.

Hardison taught me that the most important person being my word matters to is myself. If I don't trust that I will do the things I commit to doing, I will never trust that I will do the big stuff I want to do in the world. I have to develop the discipline of being my word so that when I commit to something big, I follow through on it and achieve that big objective for my own betterment.

Think about this: if we ourselves are not determined to always do what we say, and we sometimes don't even think we want to, or we find excuses why we can't, then we have lost our personal integrity, and others will believe us less the next time we say we will do something. We are back in the pleasing prison. It is very tempting to say the things a client wants to hear, even if we don't know whether we can keep our promises. Our goal at Keyser is to change the business world, and the only way possible is to absolutely commit to doing what we say. Therein lies the opportunity to create self-growth and a team of unmatched strength that ultimately disrupts our industry.

TRUE INTEGRITY

There are a number of definitions of the word *integrity*. A simple definition that I like comes from the Landmark Forum: "Integrity means consistency between what comes out of my mouth and what my body does." It simply means doing what you say you will do.

As I began making life-changing choices, I learned that integrity, as defined above, is the beating heart of service. If I do not stick to my word with my clients, they cannot trust me. If I show up a few minutes late, I plant seeds of doubt in their minds. Clients cannot trust me with their big items if they cannot trust me with their small ones.

Examples of the lack of integrity abound: saying you will be at someone's birthday party and then coming up with an excuse later for not being there shows you cannot be trusted. It also shows a pattern of thinking more about yourself than others. Committing to a meeting and then rescheduling it three times, or saying you will participate in a conference call and then dialing in fifteen minutes late all show inner inconsistency as well as a lack of personal concern for others.

When I read don Miguel Ruiz's classic work *The Four Agreements*, I learned that one of the agreements I must make with myself and with everyone else is to *be impeccable with my word*. This idea once seemed silly, but now it means everything to me (and I am still a work in progress). I also realized that the lasting effects of breaking commitments to myself and others can be significant and irreversible—and not to be underestimated. Hard to do something big in the world if you, and all those around you, don't believe the "commitments" coming out of your mouth. To become successful in consistently keeping my commitments, I have found that I need to be *intentional*. Before I recognized this, it was not unusual for me to have three commitments on my calendar at the same time, and then thirty minutes ahead of time decide which one I was in the mood to keep.

One of my great joys now lies in seeing the positive results in myself and in others as I do what I say.

COMPANY CULTURE

In the past, I viewed this Principle of always keeping one's word as limiting because I felt it was rigid and gave no flexibility for the unexpected. Now I see it as a central tenet of responsible behavior. I realize that there are times when things change, life happens, and the unexpected does occur. I have come to recognize that I, as a free and responsible person, have the right to change my mind and make different commitments when needed. When this action becomes necessary, which is not very often, I clean it up immediately and make it my duty to ensure that my prior commitments are always closed responsibly and settled with kindness and integrity.

Integrity—keeping one's word—is essential for long-term success. It is developed over time, like a muscle, through commitment and practice. Your whole team can work on it together; it actually becomes an enjoyable activity when done together. Soon, your office culture will reflect the power of promises kept and of words fulfilled.

When Keyser emerging technologies leader Noah Barrasso first joined us, he had grown accustomed to being promised things at his prior firm that were never delivered. One day, I casually mentioned that I would bring him a bottle of rum I had bought in Hawaii. The next morning, he was completely shocked to see it actually sitting on his desk. After a few more times of seeing me uphold my word, Noah now knows that he can trust me, and when I tell him we are going to change the world, he believes me.

YOUR CULTURE AS A DISRUPTIVE FORCE

We want to disrupt the industry. In fact, we want to help

disrupt every industry. That is why we at Keyser work to "be our word." Our team stands out by simply doing what we say. Any company who operates by this Principle will exceed the expectations of their clients. Doing what you say gains a company a significant competitive advantage in the marketplace. When people find they can believe us to do what we say, they are not afraid to trust us. Trust is the basis of long-term, meaningful, and profitable relationships, and it starts with fulfilling the simple commitments we make.

We keep our word on the little things, and that enables us to keep our commitments on the big things. We establish trust in our relationships, and together we set huge, crazy-sounding goals, knowing that we will accomplish them.

CLIENTS AND COLLABORATORS

Being your word, I'm sure you know by now, extends not just to your coworkers and clients but also to all your interactions and relationships. In working with your various business connections, people want to know they can rely on you to deliver what you've promised, whether it means sending that email you promised by 5:00 p.m. on Thursday or bringing the bowl of fruit to the fund-raiser potluck. Your words matter.

ACCOUNTABILITY

Keeping your word is huge. If you struggle with this, don't overthink it or get overwhelmed by the concept. Start with one item at a time, and follow through on whatever commitment you have made. To make it easier, write yourself a note, or send yourself an email, or set up notifications on your calendar to make sure you remember your commitments. Engage others within your team to exchange techniques that work. Create a support system. Take the needed steps to be the best at keeping your word.

If you find out you cannot be your word, for whatever reason, contact the person you made the commitment to, whether it's a coworker or a client, as soon as you know you won't be able to keep your commitment. This conviction to be your word builds trust. Be aware of your commitments to ensure you can actually do what you say you will do.

Keyser founder Darius Green helps himself keep his commitments by implementing a strategy he calls margin. Margin means dedicating additional time to himself as a backup so that he can always be on time, even if unanticipated interruptions occur.

CREATE BUFFERS

Matthew Cummings recently sent an email at 11:56 p.m.

with the documents he had promised by the end of the day. He didn't send it at 12:01 a.m.—he sent it before midnight and proved to the client he could be trusted to keep his word. That might seem trivial to many people, but it is a big deal for us. We do what we say, and if he thought he wouldn't be able to make the deadline, he would have let them know as soon as he saw he could not make it.

If you find that you consistently underestimate the amount of time it will take to deliver a quality product to your clients, try implementing margin into your schedule. By adding 20 percent more to the estimated completion date, you will surprise most clients by delivering what you promised early. If something unexpectedly causes delay, the extra 20 percent will provide you with the cushion needed to still finish the project on time.

CREATE TRUST

Honesty is another word that is used to express integrity. Honesty is a critical component in any service or sales environment. For example, if you have bad news for a client, tell the truth. You can soften the blow by having potential solutions identified for them, but clients need to know they can trust you to tell them the truth, not to spin it to your own benefit.

FALSE REALITIES

In the business of commercial real estate, true transparency is an incredibly rare commodity. Brokers generally believe that "spinning" information to clients is acceptable in order to keep them on board until the deal closes. They fear that bad news will damage their reputations and, ultimately, their profits. So they "talk around the truth" and create false realities, just to keep the client happy and their reputations unscathed. This ploy is shortsighted, to say the least. For long-term, sustainable success, I believe that truth always wins.

To me, bad news early is good news, and bad news late is terrible news. Providing unfiltered bad news as soon as you become aware of it engenders trust; waiting and hoping you can "fix" bad news destroys trust. I have seen many brokers get fired for trying to "shield" clients from bad developments. We at Keyser have learned that you create positive perceptions and trust by being honest, even with hard truths.

A while ago, Robert Harding, one of our rising stars, was in the beginning stages of serving a new client and promised a number of deliverables to the client by the end of the week.

As the week passed and other things interrupted his plans, it became evident that we likely would not be ready on time. As soon as he realized he wouldn't be able to get the client the best possible deliverables by the deadline, Robert contacted the client and let him know we were running behind. Rather than being upset or frustrated, the client greatly appreciated our honesty as well as our decision to take the extra time to make sure the materials reflected excellence. The result of Robert's honesty was solidifying our relationship with the client.

Of course, this kind of honesty may occasionally cause you to lose clients. In my experience and opinion, however, those are often not the clients you really want. It is important to be thoughtful about what commitments you make and by when so that you can give yourself enough time to deliver them. Otherwise, you are always scrambling to restructure your commitments, which is unnecessarily stressful.

The rewards of being honest with your clients will come back to you in spades. You cannot claim to be of service if you are not speaking the truth.

COMMIT TO FLEXIBILITY

When you are truly selflessly serving people, you will find that needs sometimes occur at inopportune times. Committing yourself to being flexible is the only way you will be able to take advantage of these unexpected opportunities. This does not mean, of course, that you must be at the beck and call of overly needy clients, because it is important to protect your own time and maintain your sanity. However, a flexible mindset does allow you to be of genuine service when someone truly has a need.

Ideally, our relationships with clients will last for years or even a lifetime. Keeping our word in business deals increases our probability, in exponential measures, of gaining and keeping these long-term relationships. A person of integrity and honesty builds lasting trust and success, both for their business and for their life.

KEY PRINCIPLE POINTS

1. Be your word. Do what you say you are going to do. This commitment builds onto the Principle of taking on only the projects you know you can do with excellence.

2. Integrity is consistency between what comes out of your mouth and what your body does.

3. Going along with the excuse that "everybody does it" only contributes to the lowering of your personal standards and the value of integrity. Disrupt social definitions by being your word.

4. Balance the protection of personal time with the willingness to be flexible in order to meet the needs of others.

5. Set reminders for your commitments, and maintain good communication with your clients.

6. Add margin to your estimated delivery dates to help account for unexpected interruptions and ensure on-time deliverables.

7. Integrity, honesty, and flexibility go hand in hand.

8. Building trust in the little things shows clients you can do the same with the big things.

BOOKS TO GROW BY

The Four Agreements by don Miguel Ruiz

This is better than any other book I have read on the subject of "being your word." The first agreement listed by Ruiz is to be impeccable with your word. He explains how powerful it is to do what you say, say only what you mean, and never use your words to hurt others. Being your word enables others to trust you, which is essential to accomplishing your big goals.

Extreme Ownership by Jocko Willink and Leif Babin

Using Navy SEALs as examples, this book asserts that taking ownership for everything under our responsibility is ultimate power. Willink and Babin describe the ultimate benefits of being one's word—not blaming others when things go wrong but taking responsibility for EVERYTHING—and as such, being the trustworthy leader that others can trust and follow.

HAVE FUN

"We have fun with what we do and with the members of the team. This is a mission we are thrilled to be a part of, and we won't take on a client unless it will be fun for everyone. Nothing is worth sacrificing our happiness over, and so we are lighthearted and playful in all we do."

SELF

As we were sitting together, creating and refining our core operating Principles for Keyser, founding Keyser member Ian Davie said, "All these Principles so far are so serious... We need to put one in here about having fun!"

"So true," I said, and Principle 9 was born, reminding us to stay lighthearted and have fun in what we do. With so many solid, serious Principles in place, he knew we needed to make sure that joy would be a part of our team. He was right, and today, this is one of my favorite Principles.

In Principle 7, I talked about one of the main questions we encourage people to ask themselves: "Is this activity bringing me joy?" Service must be voluntary—it can never be a requirement imposed by someone else. A person's service must be authentic, coming from one's own heart, where it is fun to serve.

Like many of these Principles, having fun is a mindset and it is a created space for a person to operate from. I choose to have fun, even when things are overwhelming and scary. Choosing to have fun and be lighthearted and playful helps me respond more effectively to whatever I need to handle in that moment. Over time, it enables me to actually enjoy the experience of creating a company and changing the world versus stressing and worrying the whole time.

COMPANY CULTURE

In business, being effective does not equal being serious. The humorless mindset of "come on, people, let's get serious" leads to a culture of fearful and unhappy employees. Being "serious" leads to depression over failed proposals and despair over lost business, coupled with the ever-present blaming attitude. All this produces a grim and unpleasant office atmosphere in which employees are afraid of their bosses and dread going to work.

AT WORK, AT PLAY

We maintain an ever-present spirit of playfulness and fun within our office as a vital part of who we are and what we do. We integrate social activities to meet and involve one another, tossing footballs and rubber ducks around the office, having Ping-Pong, golf, and video game competitions, and handing out crazy awards—we're generally quite the silly bunch. We have a company basketball league, engage in cheesy competitions such as wall squats and push-up contests, bring in funny comedians as birthday traditions, and pass a lint roller around as an award for saying something that makes everyone laugh.

THE ORIGIN OF THE DUCKS

Keyser had a humble beginning. To get our start, we shared a space in the back corner of an architecture firm. Someone had left a rubber duck in our area. At first, we started tossing it back and forth, and then turned it into an award for the person who said something to make us laugh. We realized we enjoyed throwing it around in the open cube environment and we could toss it without hurting anyone or breaking computer screens.

Pretty soon we were ordering rubber ducks in bulk, and now we use them to get each other's attention, shoot hoops, or have all-out duck wars. Today the duck is our official mascot and a visual representation of our company's personality.

THE DEEPER MEANING BEHIND THE DUCKS

FUN: Rubber ducks act as our reminder to have fun wherever we are. While we act as we are—the best in the business— we strive to make every experience enjoyable and never take ourselves too seriously. In a business as intense as commercial real estate, it is always fun to watch people gaze in wonder at the ducks everywhere as they tour our offices.

RELAXED & WORRY FREE WHILE WORKING OUR BUTTS OFF: Ducks on the surface always appear calm, cool, and collected, but below the surface they are furiously pumping their legs. We too want to be calm, cool, and collected regardless of what is going on around us as we work hard to create success for ourselves and others. Worries and problems roll off us like water off a duck's feathers, and we seek to be unrattled and peaceful in all we do.

TRUE TEAMWORK: If you have ever watched ducks flying in a "V" pattern, it is a wonder to behold. Ducks work as a team to conserve their energy and together they cover more distance than they could on their own. Ducks demonstrate that the true sum of the parts is much greater than the whole. They truly are one team.

SELFLESS LEADERSHIP: The lead duck has the hardest job. Not only must it set the course and the pace, but it encounters the highest wind resistance. The lead duck truly embodies servant leadership and leads with action. That is the Keyser way.

EXTRAORDINARY EFFORT LEADING TO SUCCESS: If anyone has ever observed a duck taking off into flight, you cannot be anything but impressed by the effort involved. Flight takes a similar amount of effort as success through selfless service.

SELF-IMPROVEMENT: Ducks constantly prune themselves to remove parasites, scales, and reapply the waterproof oil onto their feathers. This duck lifestyle is a good reminder for all of us to consistently focus on self-improvement.

For all these reasons and many more, ducks are very near and dear to us at Keyser and you will see them scattered around our offices and throughout all of our materials. Simply, ducks remind us of what's truly important.

See the Keyser ducks in action, #6 in the vault:
www.ruthlessbook.com/vault

I walked into the office one day to find Cooper Sutherland, one of our senior project managers, and Greg Leight, one of our key team members, heads down, focusing on a project, looking stressed out. I said, "Whoa, whoa, whoa! You guys look way too *not* Principle 9 right now," which, of course, led to a number of our rubber ducks flying around the room and a significant lightening of the mood. When you work, you can be intense and serious, of course, but be lighthearted about what you are doing and remember to smile and have fun!

Stress shuts off creativity. Every time you get worried and stressed, it makes the task at hand all that much harder. The more intense a project, meeting, or situation feels, the more important I believe it is to bring a light-hearted attitude to it. Nothing is usually ever as serious or stressful as it appears. Approach your business with a commitment to being happy and productive, clearing your mind of stress so that you can do the task to the very best of your ability and have fun doing it. What is the worst thing that can happen?

Remember to be grateful for all that you have and do your best with a good attitude, and the rest typically takes care of itself.

Although we are very committed and serious about one another, our clients, and what we do from a business standpoint, how we do it is lighthearted and playful, always remembering to enjoy our time together as a team.

CLIENTS AND COLLABORATORS

How can anyone feel positive, hopeful, and ambitious and be upbeat in interactions within the business community when they are constantly afraid? How can a person take risks to go above and beyond for clients when they feel the need to be overly cautious, fearful that their work will be ridiculed or belittled? Business is intense enough. I want our people to be lighthearted and playful in all we do. If we lose business, great. That business wasn't meant for us. Business people tend to take everything so seriously and act stressed so much of the time. I choose to look at business as a game, and as a result, it becomes more fun, and we win more.

We want happy, productive people who are giving their all and are serious about achieving optimal results for our clients. We make our work fun and we refuse to take ourselves too seriously.

RESPECT AND VALUE

Another important element of this Principle is protecting our people from abusive behavior from clients. In a highly competitive, service-oriented business like ours, it is somewhat common for clients to view their brokers as a commodity. As such, it has been my experience that many clients, partners, or collaborators can act with unkind, dismissive, or abusive behavior toward brokers in the name of a potential transaction. At Keyser, we refuse to work with partners or clients who think of us as a commodity, mistreat us or take advantage of our generous and giving spirit.

Our first commitment is to our team. We will (and have) fired clients who treat us poorly or do not respect our value and commitment. We choose our clients based on mission and purpose alignment first and profitability second. In a ruthless industry like we are in, there is no end to potential clients who wish they could find a trustworthy, committed brokerage team to serve them. I want to work for those clients rather than waste my people's valuable time and energies with those clients who are self-absorbed, abusive, and disrespectful.

Taking on a client for us is intentional and always a choice. We work with a client only as long as there is mutual respect and only as long as we are able to help and add value. We do not have a desperate "have to have this business" mindset. We purposefully choose those with whom we will work and those with whom we will not. That keeps it fun and light.

IT'S NOT A BEAUTY CONTEST

As a general rule, we rarely answer requests for proposals (RFPs). RFPs tend to be highly competitive beauty contests, and they insinuate to some degree that all commercial real estate brokerage firms are the same. These auction-type bidding wars are mainly designed to encourage providers to lower their fees until very little profit, if any, is left. This isn't the kind of business we want to participate in.

Therefore, except for very rare occasions, we decline to participate in beauty contests of this kind. There are plenty of other firms out there who are willing and delighted to participate. In fact, it is relatively commonplace for brokers to brag that they have been invited to answer an RFP to "compete for a piece of business." Not us.

When we meet prospects face-to-face, we are usually able to tell very quickly whether or not we are a good fit for them. Rather than pitch, we get to know them, listen intently to them, and ask a bunch of questions to determine whether we believe we can help them. Once they get to know us and our approach and deep service mindset, if they still are not sure that they want to hire us, we are most likely not the right fit for them. And that is 100 percent okay with us.

Our internal team at Keyser understands this. Retail industry veteran Mark Leblanc puts it well: "When we decline to take on a client and the associated revenue because they don't look at us as a partner, we save our time and energy and are able to then create a profitable business relationship with someone else."

When team members see their leaders saying no to business opportunities that might cause them to be abused and underpaid, they feel valued and empowered. We do not have to go along with every deal that presents itself, and we do not have to chase the money. There are other more important considerations, such as happiness, fulfillment, purpose, and a safe and fun work environment. The best part is, by turning down the abusive or unprofitable clients, our brokers can make more money, and they are happier doing it.

Because we value choice, anyone on our team can turn down a job or client without fear of punishment.

Whenever anything in the office is causing grief—a client, a collaborator, or another team member—we deal with it *fast*. Our goal is to be lighthearted and happy in our business dealings, both internally (in the office) and externally (in the business community).

ABUNDANCE OF PARTNERSHIPS

One example of how we protect our culture of fun is that we choose to be inclusive, not exclusive, in our relationships with partners and collaborators. We realize that there are plenty of referrals to go around for those who understand the concept of wealth through service. We believe that people will always refer business to those who have best served them. For this reason, we can work with multiple referral partners within the same field, adding more value to *all* of them and having fun while doing so.

Early in my career, a prominent corporate attorney voluntarily introduced me to a number of his top competitors. He showed me that he cared more about introducing me to people who could help me than about the possibility of my referring business to someone other than himself. He cared only about helping *me*, with no concern for his personal gain. Not surprisingly, he continues to be the top biller at his firm and one of the top producers in the state. These openly collaborative people are the ones we enjoy working with.

Taking business too seriously evolves over time into a mindset of cynicism and pessimism. We all know people who have grown angry and bitter after years in the workforce. They complain that the world of business is brutal and vicious, and they are usually right. By contrast, we choose to make our work environment a pleasurable place for team members and clients alike.

With our focus on fun and enjoyment, we find freedom to be ourselves. At his previous firm, Matthew Cummings recalls how he would stress out over emails to clients because he was concerned he would get in trouble if he said the wrong thing, had the wrong tone, or created the "wrong" impression with a client. As a member of Keyser, he gets to be his authentic self, speaking without fear of repercussion in a way that is comfortable and natural for him. This empowers him to speak the truth boldly, which creates closer client relationships because there is a genuineness in his communication that gives his clients freedom to also be themselves. Relationships like Matthew's are professional but feel friendly because they are relaxed and fun. They are more like friendships than business connections.

Having fun permeates our whole organization. A commitment to having fun with all we do, respecting our own value, and refusing to allow ourselves to be mistreated, gives us the freedom to be authentic. It has created a fun, collaborative work environment. As the successful entrepreneur Richard Branson says, "I don't think of work as work and play as play. It's all living."

KEY PRINCIPLE POINTS

1. Brainstorm on how to have more fun wherever you are and with whatever you're involved in. Find ways to enjoy your time at work and at home—they are both a part of life. Why waste them?

2. Create a fun environment. Find ways to involve and encourage the team with games, awards, and tactics for lightening the mood when the environment becomes unproductive.

3. Don't be afraid to fire clients who treat you poorly or do not respect your value or commitment to them. Relationships with clients should be mutually respectful and enjoyable.

4. Choose your clients based on mission and purpose alignment first and profitability second.

5. If anything in the office is causing havoc or grief, deal with it *fast*. Problems like this can spread quickly within your team and can hurt the culture you've worked so hard to build.

6. Being inclusive, not exclusive, will build value in your relationships with partners and collaborators.

7. Allow people the freedom to be themselves. Authenticity will create relationships that incorporate a level of friendship between the team and their clients.

BOOKS TO GROW BY

The Rise of Superman by Steven Kotler

This book describes how joyful stress-free contemplation produces extraordinary creativity. When we relax, have fun, and strive toward a mission that we are passionate about, we achieve a new level of performance and we maximize our potential. I love how this book emphasizes living joyfully in the moment and achieving greatness while doing so. A similar book is *Stealing Fire* by Steven Kotler and Jamie Wheal.

The Happiness Advantage by Shawn Achor

Achor turns conventional wisdom on its head relative to hard work and happiness. Conventional wisdom says that people must work miserably hard for twenty-five years or longer, until they achieve success and can finally be happy. By contrast, Achor says that happiness is the *beginning* point on the road to success. His observation is that a consistent positive mindset is essential to achieving success, whether in business or in any other area of our lives.

INCREASE YOUR SUCCESS THROUGH SELF-IMPROVEMENT

"We invest in our own self-improvement, always striving for greater awareness of ourselves, for we know that as we align with our true identity and remain focused on our purpose that the power within us will manifest and create our highest potential."

SELF

The one thing I am addicted to over everything else is self-improvement. This is because I know that the more I do to improve myself, the better I become at everything I do. Seems almost too simple, but self-improvement is the ultimate long-term success strategy.

It is not easy, however, which is why so many people don't do it. It requires you to look honestly within yourself and take full responsibility or ownership for your own life and situation. There is something humbling and empowering about taking ownership of everything in your life, realizing that the power to change and improve is within your own reach.

Some people prefer to be victims and blame others, circumstances, the weather, or God for situations in their lives that they do not like or understand. It is truly a humbling moment when you finally realize that all the unhappiness in life—all our problems, job stresses, and relationship issues—*all* of them are there because we ourselves are allowing and creating them. They are the results of our own thoughts, beliefs, attitudes, and personal choices.

Becoming aware of less than ideal attitudes or behaviors we have that are negatively affecting our performance is the first step toward changing them. It takes courage and humility to see ourselves as we truly are, but doing so helps us identify where we can improve and gives us access to greater performance and accomplishment, not to mention joy and fulfillment.

BOOKS TO SHIFT PERSPECTIVE

A very helpful tool for self-improvement is reading great

books. Reading expands your mind and is transformative to your thinking. With so many distractions in the world, finding the time to sit and read is very difficult. However, by making an intentional commitment to reading, and *making* the time for it, you will find much-needed assistance and lots of good advice. I find it is one of the fastest ways to stand on the shoulders of giants and learn best practices that otherwise would take me years of trial and error to learn.

Modern technology offers us many ways to make this commitment much easier. We have audiobooks, You-Tube videos, and podcasts for all types of reading. If you happen to need a place to start, jump to the great resource books listed at the end of each Principle. Each one is available in an Audible version.

Most successful people are also good readers. When you meet people whose success you admire, ask them for the names of the top two books that have most impacted their lives. Check those out for yourself. Also, when choosing books, be sure to explore both older works and current titles to give yourself a good mix of both past and present wisdom.

Reading is a golden opportunity to interact deeply with those who have traveled the path before us. I take advantage of every opportunity I can to read. I read a lot, and I always try to quickly put what I learn that can help me into practice. I maximize these opportunities to better myself. I think of reading as an investment in myself. Others may think of reading self-improvement books as boring or a waste of time and energy. But successful people make the time and put forth the energy to do what others consider too laborious.

Every book you read expands your thinking and helps you discover things about yourself you may not have considered before. Reading will challenge you and change you. I have read the stories of many successful people, and nearly all of them have consistently read good books, taken development courses, and sought out mentors in a relentless effort to improve and grow.

My questions to young people who want to be successful are, "What are you doing to improve yourself? Do you seek out good books and courses? Do you put into practice the good advice you discover?" This, in my opinion, is the best predictor of future success.

One book that has been incredibly valuable on this topic is David McRaney's *You Are Not So Smart*. It shifted my view of myself and how I interacted with others. It helped me a lot. So, even if you think you are too busy, take the time to read; it will enrich your life, and your relationships and business ventures will profit as well.

COMPANY CULTURE

We all need change in our lives at some level, especially when working with a team of people who, though they all have similar goals, are simply different people.

It is futile to pretend we are perfect. No one is. Don't react to a critique as though it were motivated by malice, and don't play the victim and blame everyone else for your problems.

For those who truly want to be great, everything in your life is subject to change and open for improvement. I choose—rather than resist—feedback and actively seek it out from others around me. I want to know where I can improve so I can get better and be more effective.

Rather than seek out self-improvement, however, many people spend their lives creating a protective environment around themselves, resisting loved ones or team members who are brave enough to give honest feedback. As a result, many people go through life never changing the same self-destructive behaviors that are sabotaging their own personal success and happiness. If they would listen to others around them, they would realize they should change, thereby dramatically improving their lives for the better.

We all have "blind spots," and we need others to reveal

them to us. Do not discount or discredit the feedback of others, even if it hurts and sounds critical or like it is coming from a mean place. Do not reject, attack, or remove from your life those who tell you the painful truth.

Most of us have an automatic internal defense mechanism that immediately lists in our minds all the reasons why any criticism levied is invalid. Our self-talk has ready responses for all negative feedback, and we can quickly come up with reasons why what we are doing can't be helped or is right and justifiable. We rationalize by telling ourselves that the criticizer does even worse and they do not understand, or have no idea how hard it is for us. As a result, we miss the priceless opportunity to grow.

Listening humbly to feedback and then embracing it gratefully and courageously lets us discover things we may not have otherwise seen. With this new awareness, we are able to make changes needed to grow and create new levels of success. This is what a good company culture provides. A safe place for everyone to help one another self-improve without fear of ridicule, retaliation, or retribution. It is one of the most important parts of creating a culture of selfless service.

COURSES TO GIVE DEPTH

In addition to books, there are many practical courses you

can take to help improve in the different areas of your life. There are masterminds, executive forums, meditation offsites, parenting courses, spiritual retreats, financial courses...The list of opportunities for growth is endless. As a leader, ask yourself, "Have I created a culture of self-improvement, and have I modeled it?" We live in an era where the wisdom and insight gained by others throughout history is accessible to us with one tap on a screen. Are you taking advantage of this unprecedented access to knowledge, or are you living with your head in the sand, complaining about how hard life is?

Before he worked at Keyser, Noah Barrasso had hit a plateau at his previous company. That's when I gave him his first self-help book, *The Story of You* by Steve Chandler. Now he tells us that this led him to become addicted to his own personal growth. It started his journey of personal and professional improvement, reading countless books and attending personal development programs. Through his personal refining, he has grown to become an amazing leader in our company. He now lives the Keyser Principles as well as anyone and is responsible for ensuring, along with me, that we never lose our special culture.

CLIENTS AND COLLABORATORS

Part of how I serve people is to help them with their own personal development journey. I have had thousands of conversations coaching clients, collaborators, and partners on personal matters. I have sent out thousands of self-improvement books as gifts to others, and I have had many a serious executive crying on my shoulder about different challenges they had going on in their lives.

The only reason I am able to help people with their personal growth is because I spend so much time on my own. I walk the path with them, and I constantly listen for the pain in others so I can find ways to truly help them at the deepest levels.

COACHING

I also highly recommend that anyone who wants to take their growth to the next level hire a good business coach. This is not a move for the faint of heart. A solid coach will challenge you, push you, and hold a mirror to your face so you can see all the imperfections you need to overcome in order to achieve your goals.

ACCOUNTABILITY AND INTENTIONALITY

With this step, be cautious and careful whose voices you listen to. My experience is that many people who do not understand your vision and motivation will unknowingly try to discourage you as you become more successful, particularly people to whom you are close. They don't typically do this intentionally, but if you listen to them, you will never accomplish what you are capable of doing.

Pick the people who actually *live* the advice they give and who have the lives or success you want, and listen to them. Do not listen to the opinionated people who don't love their lives and who spend their time griping and complaining.

As I began to build my business, I found myself being told repeatedly that what I was doing was not going to work. It is extremely difficult for anyone to keep going when they are constantly hearing discouraging comments— unless they are crazy-committed and fill their heads with the right input through books, podcasts, coaching, and other positive means of input. Having a coach helped me immensely, encouraging me weekly and keeping me accountable. He helped me think through challenges as they arose and helped me keep my hope alive and my feet moving forward.

A good coach will do the same for you. Finding the right coach is critical and will play an important part in defining your future. Here are some tips to get you headed in the right direction.

1. Seek out people in your area who are doing things in life that you admire and who are experiencing

extraordinary success. Ask them who their mentors were. The more you ask that question of the successful people you encounter, the more you may hear the same names over and over again. These are the talented coaches and mentors in your area, the ones to seek out for help.

2. Choose a coach wisely. A coach is going to be molding your mindset. Be prudent in deciding to whom you will give this immense power. Choose someone who embodies what you wish to become.

3. Research them. Interview them. Make sure you are in alignment with their perspective and approach to life. Look at other clients of theirs and see if they have the results you want in your life.

Once you have chosen the right coach, work on becoming fully coachable. This will not be easy. Your coach may say things that sound unfair, judgmental, or perhaps may even hurt your feelings. Tough love from a trusted person enables you to make the necessary and desired changes. Ask yourself how badly you want to hear the truth and truly change. Force yourself to listen intently to critiques and instructions. Adopt an attitude of nondefensiveness and absorb the truth for yourself.

Being coachable eliminates wasted time and money, and it keeps you humble. Determine to walk away from every meeting with your coach with three things: a plan of action for making your desired change, a method of accountability, and a determination to carry out the plan.

As you teach yourself through practice with your coach to be more open to feedback, you will find your mind gradually opening up to the invaluable help of others as well, and you will hopefully experience less defensiveness and self-justification in a way you have not experienced before.

It can be slow, painful, and hard work, despite your deep desire to improve. Personal transformation is not an easy process. Much of the time, it will be three steps forward, two steps back. Over time, the concepts will start to sink in and you will begin to experience the change you want.

Speaking from experience, I can say that the more I allowed myself to be coachable, the more I started to figure out why some parts of my life were not working and why I was not as effective as I wanted to be. The more I listened and adopted my coach's recommendations, the more I continued to improve. If you are coachable, you will experience the same.

Having a coach can also help you to maintain a proper perspective. Good coaches can see you objectively and will remind you, when you need it, that intermittent setbacks are part of the positive progress desired. Their feedback is invaluable if you are relentless in your desire to grow.

Many people who hire a personal coach actually double or even triple their incomes. I have seen this happen with people I know. It is difficult to be vulnerable, but personal improvements greatly affect the success of our business endeavors.

As a young man, Blake Hardison resolved to "step up to the next level," and he decided to hire his dad, Steve Hardison, to coach him. As you know from reading my experience earlier, Hardison coaches high-achieving CEOs, actors, athletes, and thought leaders from all around the world. Steve charged his son the same amount for this coaching that he would charge any other client at the time. He did not do this because he needed his son's money; he did it because he wanted Blake to have the same super-high level of commitment that his other clients had. Blake took this coaching seriously, and after finishing their work together, he had already doubled his income and was positioned for exponential growth and success going forward.

Coaches are there to help you develop a mindset of constant improvement. Remember, this is a lifelong process for you and for those at your company. Growth is a mindset, not an overnight decision with immediate results. Commit to it, never give up, and your success will increase because of it.

KEY PRINCIPLE POINTS

1. Be intentional and relentless about your own self-improvement—read books, attend personal development programs, and seek feedback from others on where you can improve.

2. Accept criticism with courage and humility. Take ownership of becoming the best you can be. Keys to success are being offered free of charge in the form of feedback from others.

3. Embrace your imperfection, and be willing to be vulnerable. When you do these things, you have taken the first steps toward being coachable and becoming a vital and malleable asset to your team.

4. Consider the invaluable investment of partnering with a coach. Finding a coach who shares your values, knows your field or industry, and who has a proven track record of coaching successful people can help you get to the next level.

BOOKS TO GROW BY

Reinventing Yourself by Steve Chandler

This is one of the better books that helped me on my self-improvement path. I have read this book numerous times, and what it does best is to show the difference between a victim mindset and an ownership mindset. By taking responsibility for the problems in your life and taking action to change your behavior, you can move forward in your journey toward personal and business success. This book has changed many people's lives, including my own.

The Three Laws of Performance by Steve Zaffron and Dave Logan

For anyone interested in self-improvement, this is a must-read. The authors describe three laws of performance which, when applied, will free a person from what is holding them back and will elevate their achievements to levels they never dreamed possible. This is a book you need to read more than once. I recommend rereading it about once every eighteen months. There is so much material here that the more you grow, the more you get from each new read.

TREAT YOUR PEOPLE LIKE FAMILY

"We are a family, and always protect and serve each other. In love, we hold each other accountable through authentic, honest, and kind discussion. We are fiercely loyal to each other, and we love and care for each member of the team at all times simply because they are family."

SELF

Being able to invite people into a relationship takes trust—something not easily extended for many people, especially in a work environment. To a large extent, there's a parallel between inviting people into your fictive "family circle" and embracing those in your own family. Loving and serving people is the very basis by which trust is built, whether within your own family or the family you build within your company.

Simply put, who you see and treat as family is up to you.

My experience is that I want to view *everyone* within my company like family. I do it for a very simple reason: no one is going to feel like family within a company unless the leaders treat them like family; and as a leader, you are going to have a hard time treating people like family unless you *view* them as family. Thus, as a leader, creating a family culture starts with you and your willingness to extend your view of family to everyone in your company.

COMPANY CULTURE

People crave camaraderie and want to be loved, accepted, and nurtured. They want to wake up in the morning knowing they are part of something special.

For some, it may seem unnatural to think of one's coworkers as family, but for us, it is a critical element of who we are. We love and respect one another, and we also work together toward a common goal—two vital components that connect us with a strong bond.

BUILT ON TRUST

People who come to us from other commercial real estate firms find our culture at Keyser to be a refreshing change. It is an environment built on trust. When new brokers start here, they are told, "You are part of the family now." That doesn't mean they have to stay with us forever, of course. But once they join our team, they and their families become our family. Furthermore, the bond is permanent, no matter whether they stay for many years or have to leave within the first year. We are always here for them.

CREATING COMMON BONDS

One of the best ways to build a family atmosphere is to start at the beginning and be very careful who you add to your team. Part of what makes Keyser feel like a family is that our hiring process is focused entirely on ensuring that everyone we hire feels included in the camaraderie. Therefore, we make sure that everyone we hire shares our mission of changing the business world through selfless service. We all come from different backgrounds and beliefs, but we all share this common bond, and that makes us family.

Because we do not punish mistakes when they occur (Principle 3), the bond among our members is even stronger. This "family bond" enables us to honestly, but kindly, hold one another accountable to our goals and Principles. We never have to "walk on eggshells" or sugarcoat our observations.

DRAWN TO OUR TEAM

Chelsea Austin left commercial real estate years ago because of the culture at a previous company. "I had chosen the medical subsector of our industry because I wanted to feel like I was helping people have access to medical care. Unfortunately, the culture at the other commercial real estate firm was more about the money and commissions than about helping anyone. I got so disenfranchised that I left for another line of work. It wasn't until I learned about Keyser and met with them to see what they were doing that I got excited again about reentering the industry. After joining Keyser and getting to know the Keyser team, I felt like I had finally found my professional family. It's a family of support and energy that doesn't exist anywhere else in the brokerage world."

Mike Hirth, an industry veteran, previously owned and operated his own brokerage firm but joined Keyser because he loved the Core Operating Principles and had always felt something lacking in being on his own. "Keyser feels like family because everyone has your back," stated Mike. "That's very unusual compared to traditional brokerage firms. Within the industry, there's a lot of backstabbing between and within companies. There is a sense of ease, however, at Keyser, knowing that you can trust everyone and no one will ever dishonor you. Beyond that, we genuinely enjoy one another because of this trust."

As a leader, you will want to create a family culture at work. You can facilitate a family-like environment through not just company outings, games, and traditions but also an intentional decision to create an environment where everyone feels safe, welcome, and happy. Examine the dynamics and relationships in your own teams. Does everyone feel trusted? Does everyone have each other's back? What can you do to foster more trust and concern?

In too many work environments, people are treated poorly, punished when they make mistakes, taken advantage of, or used to further someone else's internal political agenda.

It makes people feel comfortable to be able to share struggles and insecurities. Here at Keyser, our team members know they have a safe place. None of us are perfect; we are all here to help and support one another.

SUPPORTING INTERESTS

Part of being family includes acknowledging that we all

have interests beyond work and serving one another in their pursuit of these passions. Founding Keyser member, Ian Davie, loves painting, and we support him to take time out of work to paint. The homemade salsa recipe of retail team member TJ Brewster that he would bring to Keyser from time to time was so good that we paid to have it bottled. TJ was excited to see his homemade recipe turned into a marketable product, and we now use it as gifts for clients.

SHARING STRUGGLES WITH COMPASSION

At one time, we had an agent at Keyser who out of the blue started underperforming and whose attendance suddenly became irregular. Normally, at any other firm, they would have read him the riot act and his job would've been on the line. But that is not how we do it here. We take care of one another.

I asked to speak with him. We sat down in a quiet room, and he immediately started bawling. His wife had become seriously ill, and he was trying to handle the medical bills, take care of the kids, and stay on top of his work. He was stressed about money, and the entire situation was overwhelming him. I gave him a hug, told him to take the personal time he needed to get her taken care of, and gave him some money to help him catch up. We are a family, and we take care of one another. We are concerned for every one of our team members. He still needed to get his work to an acceptable level, but he knew that, and what he really needed right then was a little love and support, and that is exactly what he got.

We love each member of our team as family. If someone messes with one of us, they are messing with all of us. I will protect and serve my people at all costs. Every member knows our whole team has their back, and this frees them up to operate in peace and with confidence. We are a family, and we protect and care for every member.

CLIENTS AND COLLABORATORS

When you treat your people like family, they are also far more likely to treat clients, collaborators, and the business community like family as well. It is hard not to and this leads to extraordinary relationships and client service levels that never would have been possible from a company with a ruthless culture.

Pretty neat, right?

Consider inviting clients to events that bring together your team and clients outside the professional world. At Keyser, we host an annual BBQ where we're able to mingle with our clients and their families for enjoyable food, fun, and conversation.

Find ways to connect with your clients outside the standard business dealings you have with them. Not only will that family culture be felt within your company and its people, but it also will be visible to clients, collaborators, and the community you extend assistance to and partner with.

Bottom line: treat your people like family and they will treat your clients like family, and you will have both people and clients who love your organization and don't want to leave.

KEY PRINCIPLE POINTS

1. Accepting coworkers into your "family circle" can be difficult, as it requires trust. Allow the spirit of selfless service to guide your actions.

2. Build a culture of trust and respect that creates an environment of safety and love.

3. Have loving accountability for your work family. Recognize when one of your team has a need or is struggling, and take steps to offer support.

4. Love and respect one another as you work together toward a common goal. Hiring people to the team who share those values and goals will help ensure that family camaraderie.

5. Value and protect each member of your team. I cannot overstate the importance of trust, family, and support among team members.

6. Creating a culture of service starts with you, as a leader, being willing to treat your people like family, who in turn treat your clients like family.

BOOKS TO GROW BY

Love Is the Killer App by Tim Sanders

I love this book. This is a practical read on how to truly love people and make yourself indispensable. If you follow the Principles in this book, you will make yourself a resource that people cannot do without, and they will love you like family and root for your success. In this book, nice guys don't finish last—they finish first!

Multipliers by Liz Wiseman

This book is an amazing, easy read. Packed with content but simple to understand, it describes a strategy of becoming successful by helping others become successful. A leader who does this is called a multiplier, which is a leader who uses their smarts to amplify the smarts and capabilities of the people around them. Wiseman challenges her readers and helps them learn how to become multipliers.

BE 100 PERCENT COACHABLE

"We are 100 percent coachable. We do not resist feedback, we are never defensive, and we look deep within ourselves to identify where 'criticism' could be even partially true. We find great value in the perspective of others and are fully committed to the consensus of the team."

SELF

Being 100 percent coachable is one of the hardest Principles to master, but it's also one of the most critical. As leaders, we often have the misperception that we have to act like we never make mistakes and have everything figured out.

I personally couldn't disagree more. What makes me a good leader is my willingness to empower everyone to give me their honest opinion about how I could improve. Sounds pretty simple, but boy, is it humbling and hard. Part of what makes the culture at Keyser so special is my own personal commitment to living the Principles. That means that when I miss the mark, not only do I allow other team members to call me out, but I also ask them to!

Coachability is the key to becoming the best you can become. If your people are not empowered to tell you the truth about your shortcomings, you will never become a great leader and you will never create an amazing culture. The change you seek in your organization starts with your willingness to embrace the brutal, hard truths about your own deficiencies and make the necessary changes.

A SWORD OF TRUTH

When I was a kid, I read a science fiction series about an imaginary world with a magical sword called *The Sword of Truth* by Terry Goodkind. This magical sword was the most powerful weapon in this world. Whoever could wield the sword would be all-powerful and could conquer evil. Countless individuals had tried to find and take the sword for themselves, but it was too powerful and killed them all.

Anyway, the hero in this story goes on a long journey to find the sword. He finally gets to the castle, fights through dragons and hordes of villains, and eventually reaches the room where the sword is kept. He reaches out to grab the sword...

Now, the reason it was called the Sword of Truth is that the moment you grasped the sword, you saw yourself as you really were, without the lies or false stories you believed about yourself. For the very first time, our hero, when he grasped the sword, "met" his real self with all his ugliness and faults. This raw realization had been so overwhelming for everyone who had previously tried to grasp the sword that it killed them.

However, our hero clutches the sword, hangs on for dear life, and accepts and stops fighting the truth about himself. By embracing the painful truth, he turns into the most powerful person in the land, saving the world from evil.

You have to ask yourself whether you are that hero. Do you strive to grab that Sword of Truth and accept the painful realities of who you have been and who you are now? Only first through recognition, then acceptance, and finally transformation can we move beyond that to create a new story and a new legacy.

HELP TO SEE

Opening up to feedback from others helps us to identify blind spots and enables us to make changes.

Many times, however, we get feedback that feels unfair and inaccurate. At those times, we must calmly examine what was said to determine if any part of it could be true. If the criticism is even 1 percent true, be grateful; make the 1 percent change, and ignore the rest.

Be careful, though, because your mind is preconditioned to reject feedback and find reasons why feedback from others is "wrong" in order to protect yourself. If someone gives you constructive feedback that you think is untrue about yourself, ask a couple of other people whom you trust and make them swear in advance to tell you the truth. I think you will find that much more of the criticisms you receive are rooted in truth than you wish to believe, but it is in finding those blind spots that your biggest opportunities for transformation reveal themselves.

Hardison was instrumental in helping me break through the delusion of thinking I was a selfless guy just because my business model revolved around helping other people. He was able to point out to me that my practice of service was a tactic that manipulated people to feel obligated to me.

Hear me share about my Steve Hardison experience, #7 in the vault: www.ruthlessbook.com/vault.

This was a difficult realization for me, but I am glad I embraced it because it led to a change of heart, and it opened the door to much greater success for me.

The more I grow, the more I realize how much I have yet to learn. I have trained myself now to appreciate the help that Hardison gives me to see my own dysfunction.

COMPANY CULTURE

At Keyser, everyone is open to coaching from everyone else, and each of us has the opportunity to teach one another. We are open to receiving feedback from any member of the team, which supports our intentionality in learning and growing as individuals. In looking to one another, we're able to find ways to improve and see where our strengths lie from a more personal perspective. As much as a new realization may sting, we are grateful when we identify a blind spot in ourselves because it expands our awareness and brings us closer to achieving our full potential.

COURAGE TO DISAGREE

It is also amazing how much you can learn from unsolicited criticism or advice. I have learned to listen with an open heart to the input of others rather than resisting or assuming I know best.

This takes courage, and so, to model it, I give the Courage to Disagree Award when one of our team members points out something about me that is not in alignment with our company Principles. It is empowering to encourage coworkers to be brave enough to let me know if a change is needed. This happens regularly, and I am always grateful for it, especially when it hurts the most.

This past year, at our Halloween pub crawl, a random guy standing near me intentionally slapped my arm trying to be funny, knocking my drink out of my hand. Although I did not get physically aggressive, I did get upset and yelled at him to be more careful. Later that evening, when the team was doing karaoke, a newer member of the team came up to talk with me. He said, "I want to talk to you about your reaction earlier when the guy hit the drink out of your hand. I expect more of you, and I think it is beneath you to act that way." He continued, "Normally I wouldn't say this to the CEO of the company, but you've created such an environment that I feel comfortable coming to you. That makes me feel good."

At the next team meeting, I asked him to stand up and gave him the Courage to Disagree Award to a strong round of applause. That is what being coachable is all about. I need to be coachable if I ever expect my team to do the same. It starts with the leader.

UNCOVERING THE UNEXPECTED

The other thing about coachability is you get a lot of really good advice!

If you are willing to listen to others on your team, you will discover, as I did, that they are a tremendous resource for good ideas.

Ruth Darby, a senior leader within Keyser, has added significant value to our company because she is always willing to tell me how I can be doing something better or how the company can improve.

One day, I asked her to write on the board anything and everything we could be doing better. She wrote and wrote. I implemented the things that made sense and was very grateful for her honest feedback. Most people suppress honest feedback, which limits their organization's ability to scale. I want to know every area we can improve on so we can accomplish our goals as an organization.

Changing your negative behaviors is not as hard as you think; however, identifying the need for those changes and being humble enough to accept them is difficult. Addressing blind spots pointed out by others will bring you closer to becoming your best self, and you will be able to turn more opportunities into successes.

SEE MORE THROUGH A MENTOR

As discussed earlier, having a mentor or coach could help you identify your blind spots, but they can only be helpful if you are open and coachable.

Coachability is everything. Part of being coachable is being real with your mentor so they can effectively help you. So many people struggle with this. They want to pretend that they have no problems and everything is perfect. The reality is that only if you are authentic, vulnerable, and transparent will your mentor be able to help you tackle the barriers that are standing in your way.

COACHABILITY CHALLENGES

We sometimes create specific challenges within our office environment to coach and encourage each other. One of these is the Positivity Challenge. At Keyser, we define *positivity* as speaking only those things that are affirmative and encouraging, as opposed to complaining or attacking others. It is amazing how negatively people speak, often without realizing it. By helping one another to speak positively, everyone grows together and the office culture becomes much more positive and upbeat.

As mentioned above, vulnerability and coachability go hand in hand. Being vulnerable shows others you are authentic and open to feedback. This means admitting when you mess up. If you make a mistake with a client or a team member or anyone else, be honest, and don't make excuses. Your humility will create an atmosphere of authenticity and will encourage other people to open up to you and trust you more.

Yes, grabbing the Sword of Truth is painful, but it is one of the most rewarding things you will ever do. Over time, it will gradually transform you into an unstoppable force for good. Start embracing honest criticism, and change the things that need to be changed.

BECOME A MENTOR

Another reward of being coachable with a willingness to receive mentorship is that you can become a mentor as well. I am privileged to have the opportunity to mentor members of Keyser on a regular basis, and I have created a private coaching room in our headquarters that I use consistently to help mentor and grow team members.

These one-on-one sessions are very productive. I focus

all my energy on whomever I am with as I listen intently to provide whatever that person needs. These are my absolute favorite meetings each time I have them. My team members are a priority to me; therefore, I make it a top concern to give them careful, authentic, and sincere counsel.

CLIENTS AND COLLABORATORS

Being coachable also applies to clients, partners, and business collaborators. By encouraging an environment where anyone can give you advice, you create a safe place for everyone to help you succeed. People love giving advice, and they love working with people who are willing to listen to advice.

Some of the best advice I have ever received came from business prospects. By being willing to listen to their candid feedback and make changes, they decided they wanted to work with me because they wanted a real estate partner who would listen to feedback and improve.

Additionally, by expanding the concept of personal mentoring and coaching, Hardison pushed me to consider everyone I come in contact with as another mentor, giving me the opportunity to learn from the many people I respect in the community and beyond.

Whenever I meet successful people, I ask them three main questions:

1. What's the secret to your success?
2. What have you learned through the course of your career that you might be willing to share?
3. What would you do, if you were in my situation, to think bigger and act more powerfully?

Here again, you'll be able to gain from the knowledge and experience of people who have traveled the road of success before you. They've overcome the struggles, learned strategies, and mastered various areas of business and client relations. Take their advice as gold, and glean anything you can use to succeed in your own ventures. While you're seeking advice, use the opportunity as a way to learn more about their needs so that you can continue to extend your hand in service.

Be grateful for their willingness to share their time and wisdom with you. Make sure you extend sincere thanks after you've finished your time with them by sending a note of appreciation. As I've said before, a little note of appreciation with sincerity can go a long way.

KEY PRINCIPLE POINTS

1. Have a coachable mindset, welcoming criticism. Then model it to your team.

2. Coachability is key to creating an extraordinary company culture.

3. Seek to find even partial truths in any critique. Use those truths to help you become the best version of yourself.

4. Find a mentor or coach, and be vulnerable and transparent with them. Your coach will act as a mirror, showing you your strengths and weaknesses if you let them.

5. Pick the brains of successful people all around you to see what you can apply to your business.

BOOKS TO GROW BY

Overcoming the Five Dysfunctions of a Team by Patrick Lencioni

For those leaders who are interested in being coachable and in improving themselves and their teams, this is an awesome read. The five primary dysfunctions of a team outlined in this book are absence of trust, fear of conflict, lack of commitment, avoidance of accountability, and inattention to results. These team issues all stem from the failure of leaders. To counteract these dysfunctions and implement positive changes in their companies, leaders need to be personably coachable and correct their own dysfunctions first.

The Power of Habit by Charles Duhigg

This book was very eye-opening for me. The focus here is twofold: (1) discover the unconscious habits we have that are controlling our lives, and then (2) seek to identify the bad ones and replace them with good ones. This is the secret to substantive change.

BE 100 PERCENT PRESENT

"We are 100 percent present in all that we do. We commit all of our mental energy to what we're creating and do not allow ourselves to be distracted by anything (technology, other people, or our own thoughts). We are fully present and thus maximize every action and interaction."

SELF

Think about how often conversations and activities are disrupted each day. You're having a discussion with your spouse, and you receive a text from a client. You're developing a presentation, and a friend calls to ask if you can pick something up from the store on your way over to watch the game. You are in a meeting, and your phone continues to buzz, pulling you mentally out of the conversation each time.

Distractions are inevitable. Getting back into what we were doing, especially after multiple interruptions, becomes more and more challenging and significantly hurts our productivity.

Multitasking, while a popular topic for a while, has been fully disproven at this point. A human being can only really engage their brain fully on one thing at a time without compromising their capacity to do it to the very best of their ability. If you want to be the best, you need to be fully present in what you do. Some call this the zone.

BE A GAME CHANGER

So, in a world of so many distractions, what's the solution? *Awareness and intentionality.*

Take time to notice what the major distractions are for you. While you're typing an email. While you're talking to your spouse or kids. While you're out with friends. While you're at work or on vacation. What is pulling you away from the moment at hand? Then start testing ways to block those distractions, or put them away for a time.

Mikey Maynard used to take his phone with him everywhere—meetings, dinners, family events—and he never turned it off. Whenever it made a sound, he would check to see if it was a client. It distracted him during every meeting or event he attended, and not only did it show the people he was with that they were not his top priority, but he was also not very effective because he was constantly distracted.

Today, Mikey no longer brings his phone to meetings, and he is able to focus solely on the task at hand or person with whom he is meeting. As a result, his relationships have deepened immensely, and he is able to accomplish far more than he ever could before. That is the power of being fully present.

To be 100 percent present in whatever you are doing, you may need to change your environment. Whether you are conducting a meeting, working on a major project, or writing a routine email, eliminate the distractions, both physical and mental. You will find that this will enable you to think better and create more, and you will end up with greater results. You will also see opportunities you never saw before.

MAKE YOUR LIFE AN EXAMPLE

Believe it or not, in today's world, just being fully present in a conversation can be a big differentiator. I remember being in a meeting one day with Keyser aerospace experts Karyn Macvean and Benjamin Hernandez. We were meeting with a large, multinational client who had a very complicated real estate requirement. I watched how Karyn and Benjamin remained fully present and focused throughout the entire three-hour meeting, asking thoughtful questions and taking detailed notes and never looking outside the room, at their watches, or at their phones.

After the meeting, I told them how impressed I was with them for being so present, and they looked at me, surprised. "Of course we were! That is the Keyser way," they said. "We have seen you and other Keyser members model this for us hundreds of times. We get how powerful it is, and we are committed to being a hundred percent present in all we do."

That is the power of an example.

Another example is the great Steve Hardison. I've learned a lot from watching him in this area as well. He lives up to his title as the Ultimate Coach every single day. Steve completed the Landmark Forum course as a kid, and since then, he has helped many others go through it as well, myself included. He has personally attended hundreds of graduation ceremonies and heard the same lesson hundreds of times. You would think that by now, he would be sitting in the back of the room, bored out of his mind and ready to make a quick exit. Instead, Steve does exactly the opposite. He sits in the front row and stares intently at the instructor. He listens to every word spoken, waiting for any tidbit of wisdom he may have missed the hundreds of times he has heard these same scripted lessons before.

That is being present, that is being coachable, and that is a big reason why he is such an influential person. He is constantly absorbing more wisdom from the world around him than anyone else because he is fully present in all that he does. This powerful habit is one that all of us at Keyser aspire to achieve.

Being fully present in your own life, every day, in every situation, allows you to put your full attention and efforts into that moment and maximize each and every opportunity that comes your way to the fullest.

COMPANY CULTURE

Being 100 percent present in all that we do takes commitment, practice, and accountability. As a team, we focus on learning this skill because many of the opportunities we find to serve people are uncovered this way. When meeting as a team to discuss an upcoming client meeting, being present can mean the difference between a group of distracted and unfocused people repeatedly checking their phones and a collaborative team operating at their fullest potential. Being present as a team allows for uninterrupted space where extended creative streams of thought can flow and conversations can go deeper into the intricate needs of that client. It means connections between team members and intentionality around the table.

Distractions kill a person's ability to focus and think creatively and thus the ability of a team to work together in the most productive frame of mind. Distraction is a blockade to Principle 5, "being the best," and Principle 2, "outworking the competition."

Slow down, focus on the one thing, complete it well, and then move on to the next. You will discover that you and your team can accomplish far more than you ever did trying to do multiple things at the same time.

CLIENTS AND COLLABORATORS

When we meet with a client, we allow ourselves to think *only* about that client, not about anything else—not the next meeting on our roster, not what we are having for lunch, not a fight we had that morning with our spouse, not that our kids are struggling with their homework. We shut out our own needs, and we shut off any thought we have of potential gain from this client.

We look our client in the eye and remain present at every

moment, listening intently. From this focused mindset, we are able to determine the client's most pressing needs as well as some they may not yet have considered. We think creatively about how we can meet those needs, and most importantly, we commit to following up and serving them.

My goal is to be a great listener. When anyone is meeting with me, I want them to feel like they are the most important person in the world, that I am listening deeply to every word they say, and there is no one else in existence more important than them at that moment. It is a very powerful experience to be listened to at such a deep level, and I want to give that to everyone I am with to honor them and create something great out of that interaction.

If you give the gift of being 100 percent present to everyone, you will hear people's words more clearly, you will pick up their nonverbal cues more readily, and you will ultimately understand their true needs more deeply, and then you will be able to provide them the help they need.

Our own Chelsea Austin made an intentional shift when she decided to stop taking notes during meetings. She realized that taking notes was keeping her from maximizing every interaction. Without the distraction of note-taking, she found that she was able to connect much better with clients. She can now focus on reading body language and facial expressions, which helps her understand which of her clients' needs are most critical. These nonverbal cues help her pick up on unspoken opportunities to serve her clients. She found that taking notes caused her to focus only on her own interpretation of what her clients needed rather than understanding what was most urgent to them.

Everyone is different, and I am not insinuating that no one should take notes. That said, I personally follow that practice and others at Keyser do the same. After each meeting, I grab my phone and do a quick brain-dump download of everything important that I learned in the meeting so I don't forget it. When you are fully present, it really is amazing and gratifying to see how much we can actually remember when we listen intently. We then send an email to our clients to summarize our understanding of our discussion with them. This confirms with them that we have correctly interpreted what they need, and it provides them with an opportunity to make clarifications if necessary. We use our voice memos to refresh our memories before having future interactions with them so we don't miss anything. Being fully present is powerful. Don't miss the opportunity to do so.

FOCUS THE CONVERSATION ON THEM

As a company policy, we keep our initial introductory

appointments with prospective clients focused on them. We do our very best to avoid discussing Keyser so we can focus the meeting on being about them and their needs. I find this to be unique. Most people in a service business think that a first meeting is their best opportunity to verbally throw up all over the person, talking about themselves endlessly. They use the time to tell how many great things they have done and how great they are and then talk about how they are perfectly suited to be their service provider.

I find that approach to be nauseating at best. When I am in a first meeting, the last person I want to talk about is myself. I want to hear all about them, get to know them, understand what they are all about, what makes them tick, what their needs are, and so on. I spend so much time and energy focused on them and asking questions to understand them better that we usually run out of time before we even have time to talk about us. That is great. People don't care about you and what you have done. What they care about is having someone who can demonstrate that they listen and care about them. That is the magic in any interaction.

Normally, a meeting is called to discuss one particular opportunity; however, those who practice being 100 percent present listen effectively, ask good questions, and as a result, often discover a larger and more exciting business opportunity than the one originally on the table.

One day, Darius Green was on the phone with a client who was talking to him while driving. Suddenly, she abruptly told him she had to hop off the call without giving a reason. Because Darius was fully present, he could sense something was wrong. He asked her if something had just happened, and she told him she had just run out of gas and she had to get off the phone to call AAA. Most people would have just told her they were sorry and gotten off the phone. Instead, Darius immediately asked where she was located and told her he would be right there. He drove to a gas station, got a gallon of gasoline, drove to her car, and put the gasoline into her tank so she could safely get to her destination.

Simple acts like these show clients they are a priority to you, and this is a great example of being "present" with others. That client is a client for life for Darius, simply because he was present enough on the call to pick up on a subtle opportunity to help this client when she really needed it and without her asking for it.

When clients meet with any member of the Keyser team, they sit across the table from a completely focused individual who listens intently with a heart of service, fully committed to doing whatever is in his or her power to help.

We choose to be different from others by being fully present so that people know that we at Keyser care. This is our commitment as individuals, as a team, and as an organization.

KEY PRINCIPLE POINTS

1. Do one thing at a time, remove distractions, and work diligently until the completion of the task at hand.

2. Remember that being fully present allows for free-flowing creative thought, which leads to insight and team collaboration that could bring business opportunities you wouldn't have noticed otherwise.

3. Be 100 percent present with every client. In order to hear and fully understand people's needs or positions, you need to have undivided attention.

4. Bring no distractions to and be fully present in meetings, and listen intently so the person you are meeting with feels he or she is the most important person to you at that moment.

BOOKS TO GROW BY

The ONE Thing by Gary Keller with Jay Papasan

My favorite sentence in this book is "What is the ONE thing I can do, such that by doing it, everything else will become easier or unnecessary?" Part of being present is saying no to the endless deluge of "important" things that consume our days. Get off the hamster wheel, be present in each moment, eliminate distractions, and do the important things you know will get you to your goal.

Essentialism by Greg McKeown

Similar to *The ONE Thing*, this book outlines a minimalistic approach to life and business. Minimalism means doing only what is truly essential and doing only that. Create time to sit, be quiet, and think about what is most important in reaching your goals. Then do that and do it BIG. Great success will follow.

CARE FOR YOURSELF WITH EXERCISE AND PROPER NUTRITION

"We are strong, healthy, and fit. We value and respect our bodies with regular exercise and proper nutrition, knowing it increases productivity, confidence, and our ability to be of service. We care for ourselves, and as a result, discipline flows into every aspect of our lives."

SELF

Who doesn't already know that exercise and nutrition are important? We all generally know what to do; whether we actually do it is a different story. Yet, without health, none of the other Principles contained within this book can be lived or experienced. Taking care of ourselves must be a priority if we are going to have the energy and health to be of selfless service to others.

Generally speaking, people in the commercial real estate industry value their health and fitness. However, because of the intensely stressful atmosphere of commercial real estate brokerage, we do see a big problem with artificial coping habits, such as alcoholism, drug abuse, lack of sleep, being a workaholic, and stress-eating practices. Ironically, all of these habits lead to the increased *inability* to handle stress, and they lower life expectancy for those in these high-stress environments.

Much of your ability to get or remain healthy starts with your own personal commitment. Ask yourself the serious questions: Why is being healthy so important to you? What part do my current eating and exercise habits play in my health? What do I need to change about those habits? What are my goals? What is my strongest motivating factor, and can I honestly say it is enough to keep me on track long term?

As a business person, you face stressful situations every day that fight for your attention. Proper fuel and exercise support the maintenance of both a strong body and a strong mind, giving you the ability to find balance and stay on course. Having a healthy body is essential to creating long-term, sustainable success in any industry, even more so a highly competitive one like commercial real estate brokerage.

COMPANY CULTURE

With such a strong connection between the health of the mind and the health of the body, we prioritize this Principle in our daily schedules, even when we feel too busy.

There is no benchmark that we keep—no rules that say everyone needs to be under a certain weight, maintain their cholesterol at a certain level, or whatever. This is not about trying to control people's lives. This is a mindset. We understand that good health is important to service, and we want to maximize our opportunities. We cannot do this unless we keep our bodies functioning properly.

STRONG BODY, STRONG MIND

Focusing on achieving healthy physical goals helps Keyser's team ensure that we will be able to realize our crazy-sounding dream of changing the business world through selfless service.

We purposely create a safe, comfortable environment to lower the level of anxiety and stress common to our industry. We also create an environment that fosters and supports optimum health.

Each of us is working on improving our habits of healthy eating and regular exercise. We are each a work in progress, incrementally improving to become the healthiest versions of ourselves we can be.

Several Keyser members have previously been collegiate athletes or have spent time in the military, and they know the extremes of pushing their bodies to the limit. Kari Hartman, for example, cycles and does cardio five days a week. Industry veteran Todd Linde loves to exercise and just won the most recent Keyser health challenge. Matthew Cummings doesn't miss a day on the StairMaster, and team member Karyn MacVean loves to spin and hike after work.

MOTIVATE HEALTH

Not all of us at Keyser, however, are naturally athletically inclined. So how do we motivate ourselves to get involved in improving our health habits if we don't naturally love the gym?

We encourage healthy lifestyles in several different ways.

The most obvious is involving ourselves in physical competitions, which motivates us to stay in shape and also feeds the competitive nature within most of us. We have ongoing softball, basketball, and volleyball teams that play in city leagues. In the office, we are currently in the midst of a highly competitive Ping-Pong tournament, which at Keyser is far more athletic than it sounds. We schedule athletic activities together, and on next month's calendar, we have a 5K and general fitness challenge. This helps our whole team get involved in working toward Principle 14.

FIND A LEVEL THAT WORKS

Not everyone on our staff can participate at high levels of competition; however, we can all invest in our health, and it is easier to do it together. Rick Osselaer, fondly known as the Ocelot, is a type 1 diabetic. For him, eating healthy and exercising regularly is a necessity for life and for keeping the symptoms of his condition at bay. He was drawn to Keyser because he likes being around people who are also trying to be healthy. It encourages him to stay on his plan so that he can function successfully at work and also have a longer life with his family.

Personally, I enjoy morning hikes in the mountains. Not only do they give me great physical benefits, but they also offer me a time of peace, quiet, and reflection. I get my best ideas on my morning hikes, but I also enjoy spin classes and working out with weights.

Within the office, we have created a regular health challenge. The goal is to be the one who can lose the most body fat. It is a collective challenge for those who choose to participate. We measure each participating person's body fat and weight, and then we give an award to the person who loses the most.

Physical activity isn't our only focus for maintaining health. Our kitchen and lounge area, which we fondly call "the Pond," is regularly stocked with healthy snacks rather than just candies and sodas. We have blenders on hand for creating healthy smoothies. The monthly *Keyser Fitness and Nutrition Newsletter* is emailed out by a personal trainer to equip us with simple changes we can make to improve our health.

Our approach is not heavy-handed. People can eat whatever they want. We simply encourage one another and challenge one another by maintaining an atmosphere that supports healthy habits.

Creating a healthy work environment may look different in your office. Brainstorm about what you and your team enjoy, and schedule those activities. Get your people active, and you will see better results out of your team.

CLIENTS AND COLLABORATORS

Sports and physical activities can be a great way to meet potential clients while getting or staying in shape. Maia Arneson, for example, is an avid runner and consummate networker; she sometimes runs with other business people. As a side benefit of Maia's personal commitment to health and physical exercise, she has formed new relationships, and some of those new friends have become her clients.

Ruth Darby loves to hike, and sometimes she will invite clients to hike with her. Nothing like developing a relationship when you are huffing and puffing your way up a mountain. I love to invite clients to hike, work out, wakeboard, or go on snowboarding trips with me. We get a workout in, but equally important, we get time to bond and create a relationship.

In most instances, trust and relationships start with a simple conversation. Being actively involved in sports or any form of outdoor activity can bring you and a potential client together based on common interests. It may be that you both run charity races to raise money for causes such as leukemia, breast cancer, or children's hospitals. You never know where you might enjoy your next meeting with that client once you find out you have similar interests or a shared sports mania.

One of my clients who travels a lot tries a new gym in

every town that he visits and invites the people he's meeting with while he's in that town to join him for the workout. This enables him to stay in shape while his life-style would otherwise make it challenging to be faithful at the gym.

By being a presence of self-discipline and health in your community and with your clients and collaborators, they will see you as a person committed to self-improvement and you will have the energy and vitality to serve them to your fullest capability. That is what we strive for here at Keyser.

KEY PRINCIPLE POINTS

1. The business world is filled with people struggling to reduce stress and who often look to unhealthy habits to cope. Incorporate physical activity and healthy eating to help find balance.

2. A healthy lifestyle is important for both a healthy mind and a healthy body. Create an office environment that supports health.

3. Create a safe, comfortable environment that substantially reduces stress levels.

4. Schedule fitness activities or challenges to get your team involved and supporting one another.

5. Stock your kitchen or lounge area with healthy snacks.

6. Be a presence of health and discipline in your community and to your clients and collaborators.

7. Find ways to connect with people through shared interests in various physical activities.

BOOKS TO GROW BY

Eat to Live by Joel Fuhrman

I love the simplicity of this book. It takes us back to the basics: vegetables, fruits, whole grains, non-processed foods. Not that complicated!

The Willpower Instinct by Kelly McGonigal

Part of being healthy is not only knowledge but also willpower to act on that knowledge. This book is an eye-opener for people interested in increasing their personal willpower. It gives a lot of practical advice that has helped me quite a bit.

BE DISRUPTIVE AND EMBRACE CHANGE

"We are disruptive, we embrace change, and we are forward thinking in all that we do. We continuously explore and integrate new tools and innovations, with the goal of maximizing personal efficiency and providing best-in-class service to each and every client."

SELF

This Principle takes a courageous mindset, with a willingness to go against the flow and do things differently and boldly, regardless of how they have been done in the past. If you're reading each of these Principles and beginning to incorporate them into your life and business, you're already a disrupter. Making the choice to change your life is shifting the direction of your destiny. You're taking the reins—in your own life, in your own company culture, and in the business community.

Having a disruptive mindset is ongoing and never quits. It is constantly looking for different ways to see and do things. It is the willingness to be different, and it starts with a personal decision to never stop looking for new or better ways to do things.

COMPANY CULTURE

We are building our company to last. To accomplish this, our team must evaluate our company's current business model on a consistent basis, readjusting it to fit the changes we see coming. In today's world, that means we need to be consistently disrupting our own business model before someone else has the chance, thinking creatively and collaboratively as a team and within our culture and principles.

BE CONTINUALLY DISRUPTIVE

Many innovative companies experience an initial wave of success only to end up being sold, broken up, or put out of business by a new company that has figured out a new and better way to meet the needs of the changing industry. Many of the firms that have gone out of business started out well, thinking disruptively and creatively. But then they became complacent and overlooked the importance of continually reinventing themselves.

The pace of change has increased, and individuals and organizations that do not stay on the cutting edge of innovation will be swiftly left behind.

We understand this at Keyser and appreciate the urgency of continually exploring innovative ideas, ways of doing business, and technological advancements so that we can continue to be on the leading edge of our industry.

For example, Keyser was the first company in the world to come out with an app that puts the power of space estimation directly into the hands of the tenant. Even though the Keyser Space Calculator App for iOS is a relatively simple app, people use it around the world today to estimate the square footage needs for their companies. We are committed as an organization to be constantly creating innovative ways of meeting the needs of our industry.

A few years ago, I received an email notification that one of our senior competitors had just started utilizing social media for business. My first reaction was to laugh and call him a dinosaur in my head. We have been using social media since the beginning, along with many other tools.

However, in a sobering flash, I realized there are probably areas in which we are dinosaurs as well but don't yet recognize it. That jolting thought started me asking myself on a regular basis, "Where are we the dinosaur?" to ensure that our team continues to be disruptive in our business methods.

Embracing new technologies and figuring out new strategies keeps an organization relevant and alive.

CLIENTS AND COLLABORATORS

Keyser is on the cutting edge at the present, but in as little as a few months, we could easily slip into anonymity and irrelevance, as has happened to many companies before us. We must regularly reinvent ourselves or risk being overtaken.

Keyser's Digital Infrastructure gurus, Michael Ortiz and Patrick Wilcox, know disruption firsthand, as they help clients with their critical facilities and data infrastructure requirements. "Unlike traditional firms, here at Keyser, we are working as one team instead of fragmented groups, meaning we are completely invested in the technology needs of our real estate clients," said Wilcox. "Working as such allows us to be an extension of our client's company and forge a lasting relationship as they evolve."

Disruption comes in many forms. In an industry as siloed

and cutthroat as commercial real estate, true collaboration can be a disruptive differentiator.

RECOGNIZE SACRED COWS

One way a company becomes a dinosaur is by failing to identify and eliminate their "sacred cows." Constantly evaluate your business procedures and ask yourself, "Why are we doing it this way, and is there a better, more effective or efficient way to do it?" Don't hold on to outdated methods just because you had success with them in the past. Remember that other companies are planning and working hard to overtake and dominate your industry. Don't let your company go extinct because more progressive-thinking competitors came along and took the industry by storm. Be the progressive thinker yourself. Be creative and bold, know your clientele, and implement cutting-edge practices regularly.

Two of Keyser's brilliant advisors, Ryan Steele and Clint Hardison, applied this disruptive mindset to a deal they were negotiating. The client dealt in third-party logistics. Their problem was that their contracts were typically short-term and seasonal in nature, so the client always faced very short time frames in which to find and lease large amounts of space for their seasonal clients.

After brainstorming, Clint and Ryan came up with the

idea of combining the client's stable, longer-term space needs with their less desirable, short-term needs. In this way, if a landlord wanted to benefit from the client's long-term tenancy, he or she would also have to figure out a way to accommodate the client's frequent, but unpredictable, short-term tenancy needs. Through strategic messaging and a carefully implemented strategy, Ryan and Clint were able to reframe the deal—from a structure that landlords would typically avoid—into one that was so attractive that landlords throughout the market would aggressively compete for it. This ultimately resulted in locating multiple buildings that would not only accommodate the client's short-term needs but would also do so at terms significantly below market. The client expressed that he had never secured such tenant-friendly terms in his fifteen years of leasing space.

Take time to look at your industry. Are there any "standard" approaches to doing things? How can you disrupt that standard? How can you improve it?

GET OFF YOUR LAURELS

Perhaps your business is dominating the market right now. Great. Congratulations. But don't relax and assume that you will always dominate. Never rest on your laurels. Continually seek out new technologies, methodologies, and ideas to stay relevant and keep ahead of market trends.

Schedule creative, disruptive brainstorming sessions, either by yourself or with your staff, and analyze whether or not you are keeping up with changing trends. Sit down with people outside your company, and ask what changes they foresee. Talk to recent college graduates in your industry, and get their ideas; college graduates can be excellent resources of ingenuity. Collect your ideas, and then make sure that your company is the first to make the upgrades that are both strategic and beneficial within your industry.

A disruptive mindset enables us to stay relevant in order to provide best-in-class service to clients. Being disruptive in business is how we at Keyser continue to realize our vision for changing the world through genuine selfless service.

Resist the status quo. Embrace change. Remember that just because something worked in the past does not mean it will work in the future. Be okay with constant evolution. Choose effectiveness over the desire to "play it safe," and you will continue to win over your competition.

KEY PRINCIPLE POINTS

1. If you're taking the reins and choosing to incorporate the Keyser 15 Core Principles in your life and business, you're already a disruptor in your own world and industry.

2. Disruptive is a mindset and is constantly looking for new or better ways to do things.

3. Constantly ask yourself, "Where am I the dinosaur?" to avoid being overtaken by another disruptor in your industry.

4. Eliminate "sacred cows" by asking, "Why are we doing it this way, and is there a better way to do it?"

5. Explore new technologies, methodologies, and ideas to stay on the cutting edge of your industry.

6. Make the necessary changes to remain a dominant force in your industry.

BOOKS TO GROW BY

Play Bigger by Al Ramadan, Dave Peterson, Christopher Lochhead, and Kevin Maney

I love this book. We read this at a recent Keyser executive retreat and determined that we were *still* thinking too small about our potential, as big as we already thought we were thinking. This book recommends looking at what you are doing, seeing where you can be disruptive, and then creating a new category around that new idea. Once you create a new category, the next step is to become the king of that category. This is our strategy for growing Keyser.

Bold by Peter H. Diamandis and Steven Kotler

I love challenging books like this that encourage really big thinking. The authors recommend looking for opportunities to be disruptive and taking big, bold, and fearless action. They describe individual empowerment enabled by technology to disrupt industry, change the world, and create an extraordinary impact in ways never before thought possible. Saddle up. This book is a rocket ship.

You Are Not So Smart by David McRaney

This book is a must-read for everyone. It is disruptive to what you currently believe about yourself and the world. This book was as disruptive to me personally as any book I have read in a long time. Get ready to think differently about nearly everything you believe. This book is not for the faint of heart.

DEVELOPING YOUR OWN PRINCIPLES

"The secret of change is to focus all of your energy, not on fighting the old, but on building the new."

—SOCRATES

Our Principles hold the highest importance to us at Keyser. They **are** Keyser. Without them, we are just another real estate firm. But with them...

> **We are changing the business world through selfless service.**

By now, you know exactly where you stand. You know all about The Keyser Experience and how we create it. You have determined by now within yourself whether Keyser's selfless service methodology makes sense to you and whether it is the kind of foundation you want to build your company on.

It is time for you to take your company's future to the next level. Time to take the Principles you've learned about in Part Two and make them your own. Give them life within your company culture, and let them be the guiding force for your team as you seek to be a positive and selfless force in your community and industry.

You will likely find that the Three Levels of Reinvention taught within and most of Keyser's 15 Core Operating Principles fit naturally into your culture. There also may be elements that don't align with what you are looking to create. The process of developing the Principles that will be your compass is heavily dependent on you and your team crafting governing Principles that embody the values you want to emulate.

> *Your company principles will be the most critical piece of your successful transformation. They will need to be tailored to you and your industry.*

Whether the development process takes days or weeks, make sure the principles you commit to are at the core of who you aspire to be, and then build or rebuild your business around them.

> *Once you have your principles, it is critical to embed them into everything you do as an organization.*

Do not let them degenerate into mere statements and become nothing more than lip service. Do not let them become meaningless ink on paper. You as the leader have to live them, so hold yourself and your team accountable to doing so.

> *Be the leader your company needs, and live the principles you've now built your company around. Be the example who will blaze the path your team will follow.*

You must see your job as being the ferocious guardian of the culture you have so carefully and intentionally chosen. As the old saying goes, "A fish rots from the head," so if you as a leader do not live them, no one else will.

But your journey doesn't stop there. The success of your culture depends just as heavily on the people who make up your team.

> *Commit to recruiting like-minded team members to join you, and hold your whole company accountable to living the principles in every aspect of your business.*

When you commit to ensuring the success of your new principles within your organization, you must be ready for the challenges your team will face from within. Not everyone will naturally align with the culture you are creating. You may have to let a few people go in the process. Often, some of your most talented people will not fit into a serving culture because of their personal egos. Make the change anyway.

It is imperative that you choose culture over talent.

My experience has been that the sooner you clean house, the better. Team members who are culturally misaligned can be absolutely poisonous for your organization. This was the biggest mistake I made in building Keyser—keeping the wrong people on board for too long in an attempt to rehabilitate them. It's a difficult lesson to learn.

Your entire leadership team must be completely aligned in both living and implementing your principles.

These principles are the regulating mechanism that will guide you as an organization in facing day-to-day challenges and working together toward your goals. They will knit you together as a team.

Focus on getting every member of your team to learn your principles by heart. Make it a daily habit to discuss and review them with your team.

> *Your principles should become so well known that they get buried in the subconscious of every team member—becoming second nature to each of you.*

When you get to the point of quoting the Principles as part of normal conversation without realizing that you are doing it, that is when they have taken root at the soul level.

True success is getting to the point where all members of the team live the Principles in their daily lives. For a downloadable booklet of the Keyser 15 Core Principles go to deliverable #1 in our vault: www.ruthlessbook. com/vault.

ENGAGE WITH US

After reading this book, if you are motivated and inspired to join our Movement to change the business world through selfless service, here are three simple ways that you can join us depending on your current situation:

If you work in the commercial real estate industry and are tired of the traditional commercial real estate firm environment, call us. We are always looking for talented, best-in-class, service-oriented leaders to help open up new Keyser offices and take leadership roles as we grow Keyser to a *Fortune* 500 company. (Learn more at our site: www.ruthlessbook.com/Keyser.)

If you are an executive and you would like to experience what it is like to have a Keyser commercial real estate advisory team helping you with your real estate requirements, we would love to talk to you. It would be my personal honor to be able to serve your needs and show you a level of service you have never before experienced. Learn more about the Keyser Difference at: www.ruthlessbook.com/difference.

If you are not in commercial real estate, but are a leader in a company or industry that needs similar change, we can help. If you would like help creating The Keyser Experience for yourself in your own organization, contact us. We have lots of resources to help you create a culture of selfless service for yourself. Check out our Selfless Service Starter Series: www.ruthlessbook.com/selfless.

NOTE FROM THE AUTHOR

If you just finished reading my book and need help in this big undertaking, we are here for you. We want to serve you. We are developing the Keyser Institute to teach you how to integrate selfless service effectively into your organization. We have served thousands of leaders in industries of every variety. We have helped them create and refine their selfless-service missions. Let us know if we can help you, and keep an eye out for our upcoming book that will take you to the next level with information about The Keyser Way.

I hope the practical advice in this volume will help you move forward toward transforming your business as well as your life. I hope you are convinced that it is absolutely possible to bring a spirit of service to the business world that will end up bringing success and happiness to you as it has me.

Be blessed,
Jonathan

ACKNOWLEDGMENTS

My mom and dad for giving me life and loving and supporting me selflessly through everything, and for helping me heavily edit/rewrite parts of this book.

Steve Hardison for introducing me to myself for the very first time and encouraging and holding me accountable to BEING who I really am.

Steve Chandler for starting me on my reinvention journey and helping pull the first iterations of this book out of me.

Maia Arneson for all her extraordinary efforts in helping me get this book to market.

Everyone at Keyser for being so darn supportive and awesome.

Jerry Porter and Matthew Miller for believing in me when very few did.

David Marino for taking the time to help a young guy in the business.

Keith Ferrazzi for inspiring me and being a great friend.

Dave Squire for being an amazing mentor and friend.

John Ruhlin for being such a friend in this process.

Robyn Burwell for helping turn my vision for the book into a reality.

My precious Susanna for loving me and giving the kids and me a very happy new life.

All of my friends in the Arizona business community who believed in our vision and helped and supported us in so many different ways along the journey. We would not be here without each and every one of you, and I'm extremely grateful for all the support and love.

ABOUT THE AUTHOR

A former ruthless, cutthroat commercial real estate broker, **JONATHAN KEYSER** used to do whatever it took to win. Fortunately, he had a change of heart, launching Keyser in 2013 with the mission of reinventing and transforming the commercial real estate brokerage industry through selfless service.

Today, he is the founder and thought leader behind Keyser, which is the largest commercial real estate tenant brokerage firm in Arizona and one of the fastest growing in the country. Through his disruptive focus on selfless service, Jonathan is reshaping the commercial real estate industry, and his firm represents thousands of companies globally across multiple industries.

Considered one of the top thought leaders in the commercial real estate sector, Jonathan is passionate about helping and empowering others and is involved in many different executive and nonprofit organizations. A best-selling author, national speaker, media contributor, and strong supporter of the Conscious Capitalism movement, Jonathan is actively working toward the upcoming launch of the Keyser Institute to inspire, train, and equip the next generation of selfless leaders. He works with executives and business leaders, helping people assess and activate selflessness in their company culture.

On the personal side, Jonathan prioritizes family. Alongside his wife, Susanna, he is a loving and devoted father to his four children, three dogs, and one cat. Jonathan is extremely committed to personal development and self-improvement, and he stays active with mountain/water sports, spin, and hiking.

Made in the USA
San Bernardino, CA
18 August 2019